And God said,
"Let there be evolution!"

Reconciling the Book of Genesis,
the Qur'an, and the Theory of Evolution

Edited by
Charles M. Wynn, Sr. and Arthur W. Wiggins

ALL THINGS

THAT MATTER
PRESS

ISBN: 978-0-9846392-5-0

Library of Congress Control Number: 2011928831

Cover Design by All Things That Matter Press

Published in 2011 by All Things That Matter Press

Table of Contents

Preface

True reconciliation proceeds always by a mutual comprehension leading to some sort of intimate oneness. —Sri Aurobindo

Reconcile:
1. To establish a close relationship between
2. To settle or resolve
3. To make compatible or consistent

According to most monotheistic religions, God created the material universe and gave it order. Modern science investigates that material universe and attempts to understand that order. Although one might therefore expect that members of these religions would welcome the insights into God's creation provided by modern science universally, such is clearly not the case. Billions of people are unable to reconcile their religious beliefs with the ideas of modern science. As a result, they reject, and sometimes even attempt to suppress or eliminate, scientific ideas.

This is especially true when it comes to reconciling the theory of evolution, which, in its broadest sense, is the idea that the universe has a fourteen-billion-year history of naturalistic change through time, and religion, which teaches that the history of the universe includes supernatural changes and events, and may have occurred over a much smaller time. Evolution has been rejected by literalist Jews, Christians, and Muslims alike. A number of state and local school boards in the United States have taken an anti-evolution stance on the ground that the teaching of evolution contradicts the account of origins given in Genesis.

In 1995, in response to this dilemma, the most prominent organization of American scientists, the American Association for the Advancement of Science, established an office in Washington, D.C. to promote "Dialogue Between Science and Religion." In 1996, the Center for Theology and the Natural Sciences, which is located in California, initiated a program called Science and the Spiritual Quest.

In addition, the National Academy of Science and the National Science Teachers Association have spoken out against groups that take an anti-evolution stance. Moderate religious organizations have added their voices to those of the scientists. For example, the American Jewish Congress, Roman Catholic Church, and United Presbyterian Church in the USA have published statements defending the teaching of evolution in the public schools.

Interest in such interfaith issues is on the rise. According to a *Parade Magazine* article ("Can't We Get Along?"), "Sept. 11, 2001, is proving to be a defining hour of religion, as interfaith groups of all dimensions are thriving—and cooperating—as never before." Throughout the United States, Jews, Christians, and Muslims are meeting in increasing numbers to talk about religion. They seek mutual understanding and respect.

To provide a focal point and catalyst for these trialogues, *And God said, "Let there be evolution!"* offers perspectives about science and religion written by three scientists, each of whom participates in a different religion whose patriarch is Abraham. Its discussion of Islamic beliefs is especially significant since recent terrorist activities by Muslims willing to sacrifice their lives for what they believe to be a holy cause have put Islam in the spotlight. Islam is the fastest growing religion in the United States, and there are over one billion Muslims in the world. Shedding light on Islamic as well as Jewish and Christian beliefs should help people of all faiths appreciate these three religions more and mistrust them less.

It would be arrogant and naive to assert that the efforts of these three scientists will be the last word on the subject of science and evolution. Many who feel strongly about their own beliefs will differ from these viewpoints. Nevertheless, as Rabbi Tarfon admonished in *Ethics of the Fathers*: "It is not incumbent upon you to complete the work, yet neither are you free to desist from it."

Part One

Origins

According to the Hebrew Bible, about thirty-eight centuries ago, God made a covenant or agreement with Abram of Ur, later called Abraham: God would establish "a great nation" from Abraham's descendants. In return, Abraham and his descendants would offer the one true God complete obedience. And so, Abraham, which means "father of the many," became the first patriarch (father) of the Jewish people.

Eighteen centuries later, Jesus of Nazareth, who was born into a Jewish family and lived as a Jew his whole life, founded Christianity as a fulfillment of Jewish prophecy. About six centuries after the founding of Christianity, Muhammad ibn Abdallah founded a third Abrahamic religion, Islam.

More than half of humanity—about 2 billion Christians, 1.3 billion Muslims, and 15 million Jews—are members of these three monotheistic faiths and share Abraham (in Islam, Ibrahim) as patriarch. All three religions share beliefs with one or both of the others.

All believe in a single, all-powerful, all-knowing, caring God who somehow created the world. Although the names they give to their one God differ, all names refer to the same God. Jews refer to God as Adonai, which means "my lord" or "Sovereign." Muslims refer to God as Allah, an abbreviation for the Arabic term *al-ilah*, which means "the God."

Both Islam and Judaism teach that Abraham and his wife Sarah had a son named Isaac, who is the ancestor of the Israelites, and that Abraham and his second wife Hagar had a son named Ishmael, who is the ancestor of the Arab peoples. Jews and Muslims are thus the progeny of brothers, full cousins according to their shared traditions. Appropriately then, an oft-cited verse of the Qur'an reads: "Do you not know, O people, that I have made you into tribes and nations that you may know each other."

Revelations

According to Jews, Christians, and Muslims, the Word of God, what humans are supposed to know and do, has been revealed through human interpreters called prophets. These prophets are believed to have received divine messages in ways that include dreams, visions, and physical manifestations. Whereas some prophets, such as Moses, are accepted by Jews, Christians, and Muslims, only Muslims accept Muhammad as a prophet.

Christians believe that, in addition to revelation by prophets, God's Word was also revealed through a Messiah (a Chosen One or Christ) named Jesus, who entered human history as the Son of God to redeem humankind through His death and resurrection. They see Jesus as the Word of God in human form. According to Catholicism and many Protestant denominations, Jesus, the Son of God, along with God the Father and God the Holy Spirit, is part of God, a triune Being eternally existing in three persons.

According to the Jews, Jesus was not the Messiah they anticipated because he did not redeem the world from evil, gather all the exiled Jewish people into the land of Israel, and usher in an age of peace and tranquility. According to Muslims, Jesus was one of a number of great prophets of Allah.

Sacred Texts

Written records of these revelations form the sacred texts of the Abrahamic religions: the Hebrew Bible for Jews (referred to as the Old Testament by Christians), the New Testament for Christians, and the Qur'an for Muslims. The Hebrew Bible contains the story of how God created the world and established a covenant or testament with the Jewish people. For traditional Jews, its first five books, collectively known as the Torah (Hebrew: teaching, law), are the definitive self-revelation of God. It was written from approximately the middle of the tenth century BCE to the middle of the second century BCE.

The Christian Bible, which was written from approximately 50 CE to the early or middle 100s CE, was written for those who believed that Jesus Christ came as the Messiah as prophesied in the Hebrew Bible. It adds to the Hebrew Bible a Christian or New Testament ("Testament" means promise), which tells the story of Jesus' ministry and how he became Messiah, Lord and Savior. Many Christians see the Bible as being divine words in human language.

According to Islamic tradition, the Jewish and Christian interpretations of the Word of Allah were not in accord with the true revelation or Word of Allah preached by Ibrahim. (The Qur'an calls Jews and Christians *ahl al-kitab* or "followers of an earlier revelation.") To rectify this situation, according to one version, the angel Jibril (Gabriel) read to Muhammad the authoritative or eternal Word of Allah as preserved on a tablet in heaven, and commanded Muhammad to recite them. (Qur'an is an Arabic word meaning "the recitation.") These words, which came to him over a period of twenty years, were transcribed during the seventh century CE. They provide guidelines for living a life that is pleasing to Allah and for treating one another with justice, equality, and compassion. (Islam means "surrender" to the will of Allah.)

Together, the writings form a sort of trilogy in which the New

Testament tells of the fulfillment through Jesus of the Judaism described in the Hebrew Bible, and the Qur'an corrects, continues, and, because most Muslims consider Muhammad to be the last and greatest of the prophets, culminates the revelations of the preceding two texts. Because of this belief about Muhammad, Muslims call him "the seal of the prophets," the last messenger from Allah. A few Muslim sects, however, such as splinter groups from the Shiites, expect another prophet to come in the future.

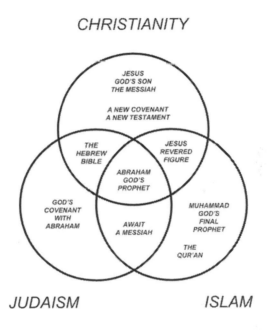

Fundamentalists

There is a small, but extremely influential Muslim sect, the Wahhabis, who fervently believe that their scripture is the inerrant, revealed knowledge of Allah. According to the Wahhabis, their concept of the truth is the one and only truth. Wahhabis adhere to a most strict, severely enforced moral standard of conduct. They were a primary force in the rise to power of the Saudi tribe of Arabs over other tribes, and the creation of an Arabian state, Saudi Arabia.

The Wahhabis are certainly not the only religious sect that claims to be the sole orthodox, correct interpreter of God's will. They are not the only group that finds it necessary to battle forces that threaten their most sacred values. They are not unique in wishing to return to what they believe are the original roots of their faith.

Fundamentalists, as such people are popularly known, are active participants in each of the Abrahamic religions. To assure that their ideas prevail, they have asserted themselves in ways that are various and sometimes shocking; for example, by murdering doctors and nurses who work in abortion clinics and by carrying out suicide missions.

Fundamentalists also reject any knowledge that seems counter to that revealed in their sacred texts. Specifically, they insist that the book of Genesis and Qur'an not only accurately express the will of God, but are also scientifically accurate in every detail.

Evolution or Scripture

Questions about the scientific accuracy of the book of Genesis and Qur'an generally focus on how the universe achieved its current condition and how the life forms that inhabit Earth achieved their present state. According to science's theory of evolution, the universe is about fourteen billion years old and Earth about five billion years old. About four billion years ago, simple life forms appeared on Earth. These life forms slowly evolved into more complex life forms that eventually evolved into a variety of species. *Homo sapiens* or modern humans appeared at least 100,000 years ago.

By contrast, the book of Genesis states that God created the universe and Earth in six days, and that during these six days, God created all variety of species or kinds, including the human species in the form of Adam and Eve (Genesis 1.1–2.3). By summing the generations listed in the Hebrew Bible, the age of the universe and Earth is estimated to be about 10,000 years.

The Qur'an states that God created the universe and Earth in six days. It attributes the origin of life to God (Qur'an 32.4–9). It also states that, after Earth was populated with other life forms, God created the first human beings, Adam and Eve.

These scenarios raise a crucial question for members of every Abrahamic religion: If the theory of evolution correctly describes the development of the universe and its life forms, is it possible to reconcile that theory with the Scriptures of your faith?

Evolution and Scripture: Three Scientific Perspectives

According to recent surveys, almost half of American scientists believe science and religion are compatible. They believe in "a God to whom one may pray in expectation of receiving an answer." Somehow, these scientists have been able to reconcile science, which attempts to explain the natural world by gathering evidence and using natural causes, with religions that rely on "revealed" truth.

To understand how this is possible, we asked three American scientists, each of whom practices a different Abrahamic religion, to explain how their understanding of the nature of science and their own religious belief allows them to reconcile the theory of evolution and Scripture.

Rabbi David E. Kay of Congregation Ohev Shalom in Orlando, Florida, a Jewish scientist who received rabbinic ordination from the Jewish Theological Seminary of America, the institution of higher Jewish learning of the Conservative movement, has a B. Sci. in Ecology, Ethology, and Evolution from the University of Illinois at Urbana-Champaign, an M.A. from the Davidson Graduate School of Jewish Education and has studied at the Schechter Institute of Jewish Studies. He has done biomedical research at the University of Chicago Hospitals and Clinics, has been a science teacher at Yeshivah Shearis Yisroel and served as Education Director of the Tree House Animal Foundation of Chicago.

Howard Van Till, Ph.D., a Christian scientist whose religious beliefs are derived from the Dutch Calvinist tradition, is Professor of Physics and Astronomy, Emeritus, at Calvin College in Grand Rapids, Michigan. He is a Founding Member of the International Society for Science and Religion, has served on the Executive Council of the American Scientific Affiliation and is a member of the Editorial Board of Science and Christian Belief. Dr. Van Till is a member of Christ Community Church Exchange (C3Exchange) in Spring Lake, Michigan.

T. O. Shanavas, M.D., a Muslim scientist, is a pediatrician in Adrian, Michigan and member of the Islamic Center of Greater Toledo and Islamic Society of North America. He is listed in Best Doctors in America and is a Fellow in the American Academy of Pediatrics. Dr. Shanavas is a member of the Center for Theology and the Natural Sciences and National Center for Science Education and serves as Vice President of the Islamic Research Foundation International.

In Parts Two and Three, each will respond to the following questions:

What scientific evidence can you provide to help convince people of all faiths to accept science's theory of evolution?

How have you reconciled science's theory of evolution with the Scriptures of your faith?

Each scientist will bring the understanding of divine revelation that he has derived from scriptures and tradition into dialogue with science. These three Theologies of Nature will reveal similarities as well as differences in their understandings about science and beliefs about religion.

If we human beings are to continue to exist as the dominant species of life on planet Earth, if we are to avoid the potentially lethal dangers associated with not being able to reconcile science and religion, it is in our best interest to focus on the areas of agreement rather than dwell solely upon the differences.

In the words of John F. Kennedy:

So, let us not be blind to our differences—but let us also direct attention to our common interests and to the means by which those differences can be resolved.

Motivations

We also asked the scientists to answer these questions:
- What motivated you to participate in this project?
- What do you hope it will accomplish?
- What benefits do you foresee from this project being an interfaith collaboration?

From Dr. T.O. Shanavas

Today in America, there is rampant hostility from the religious right to teaching the theory of evolution in public schools. They want to dilute science with the religious doctrine of Intelligent Design. If the next generation of Americans is indoctrinated with the faulty idea that science is wrong and that the evidence for evolution is questionable, this could lead to the downfall of American civilization. What happened to Islamic civilization could be repeated in America. The thought of such a scenario frightens me whenever I read anti-evolution rhetoric in the media. So, when Professor Wynn proposed this book project, I could not resist his offer to participate. I want to say to people of faith that I believe in a God who created life and that there is nothing in science that prevents me from believing in Him. Science helps us to discover how God did it. By knowing His method of creation, I become closer to God rather than parting from God. Having three different religions come to the conclusion that their scriptures do not oppose evolution will help promote open discussion of this topic.

From Rabbi David E. Kay

Dr. Mary Boyd of the Union Theological Seminary in New York taught me my most valuable lesson regarding interfaith dialogue. She pointed out that we focus most of our time and energy on identifying and articulating the common ground. This is vitally important, of course, but it is only a means of establishing a foundation for the real challenge of interfaith conversation: our differences.

If we can't talk about where we differ, even where we differ sharply and irreconcilably, we can never come to truly know each other.

I first heard about this project through a rabbinic colleague and jumped at the chance to submit my name for consideration. I found that my academic training in the life sciences, animal behavior, ecology, and evolution had only served to strengthen my sense of awe regarding the natural world. Far from undermining faith, I found that those scientists I encountered who had delved most deeply into their fields were less cynical and more, well, spiritual.

Likewise, I found that my rabbinical studies only served to confirm what science had learned, and continues to learn, empirically. I had never perceived any significant conflict between science and religion, and in-depth learning in both fields made that even clearer.

I have been involved with a fair amount of interfaith work, and given Dr. Boyd's challenge, my only hesitation was that I would be collaborating with people from other faith traditions who agreed fully with the premise of the book. We would be interacting only on common ground, an important but still somewhat superficial relationship.

Yet the impact of the harmonized voices of a Christian, a Muslim and a Jew was far too important to forego. And I was eager to hear how scientists from the other Abrahamic faiths arrived at essentially the same conclusion as I had, but within the context of their own theologies and personal experiences.

The primary value of this book is, of course, responding to the assumption that science, and evolution in particular, is at odds with religious faith. But of at least equal value is realizing that sincere people of faith, walking very different theological paths, can arrive at the same destination.

From Dr. Howard Van Till

It's quite obvious that there is a great deal of tension between modern science and large portions of the Abrahamic faith communities. This is especially so among persons not trained in the sciences, but I don't think that a lack of scientific knowledge is the most fundamental problem. Having a better understanding about how the sciences operate and having a greater knowledge of what they have learned would indeed be helpful, and major portions of this book are dedicated to that goal, but would not automatically eliminate the tension.

Why not? Many factors could be cited, but the main problem, as I see it, grows out of ordinary human resistance to the rational reexamination of cherished beliefs. This is especially true for traditional religious beliefs that we inherit as persons born into some particular faith community. This may be normal human behavior, but I believe that we all need to become more keenly aware of it so that we can more easily recognize situations where corrective measures are needed. Sometimes a new idea may need to be introduced. On other occasions we may need to correct a misunderstanding that crept into our faith tradition in centuries past.

Will reason prevail in the long run? I don't know, of course, but I believe that we need to give it our best shot and see if we can at least reduce the tension now centered on the concept of evolution. I've been at this effort for several decades and see no end to my personal involvement. It's what I do. It's what my faith heritage counts as important.

For each of the Abrahamic faiths here represented, it is essential to understand the role played by their Sacred Scriptures. Each of the scientists who have contributed to this book knows well that a continuing respect for their Scriptures must be maintained. But each of us does it differently. I find the varied approaches taken by the other two scientists to be fascinating and I am pleased to be a part of this project. As is often the case, observing how someone else approaches an important issue helps one to see and understand one's own approach more clearly. I hope that our readers will also have that clarifying experience.

Let me leave the reader with a challenge. A respected journalist once wrote: "It is impossible to reason a man out of something he has not been reasoned into. When people have acquired their beliefs on an emotional level, they cannot be persuaded out of them on a rational level, no matter how strong the proof or logic behind it. People will hold onto their emotional beliefs and twist the facts to meet their version of reality."

The challenge? Rise above this human tendency and let your mind soar into new realms of appreciation for both.

Part Two

Many Instruments, One Symphony
By Howard J. Van Till

What scientific evidence can you provide to help convince people of all faiths to accept science's theory of evolution?

One of the major scientific accomplishments of the twentieth century was the discovery that the universe has a *formational history*, a sequence of processes and events by which the basic materials of the universe came to be arranged into new forms, and that the sciences are able to reconstruct major portions of its what-happened-and-when story. Consistent values for the ages of the universe, of star systems and of the earth can be determined by a variety of methods that do not in any way depend on the concept of biological evolution. The formational histories of these physical systems are well understood as the consequence of ordinary natural causes. The scientific approach that is so successful for physical structures—an approach premised on the adequacy of natural causes—is proving equally successful for understanding the evolution of living creatures. It is becoming increasingly evident that the universe is fully equipped with all of the material resources, all of the formational capabilities, and all of the structural and functional potentialities required for the evolution of both physical structures and living organisms. We are privileged to be members and inhabitants of a "Right Stuff Universe."

I. DIVIDING A BIG QUESTION INTO SMALLER PARTS

What scientific reasons do I have for accepting science's theory of evolution? That's a great question, but it's also a very big one. It's big in the sense of including within it a long list of smaller questions, questions that I suggest we consider one at a time.

Why one at a time? Because the answers to most of the smaller questions do not depend on the way the other questions are answered. Each question deserves to be asked and answered independently, so that each response is free of any bias or prejudice that might spill over from the others.

As the reader will soon find out, I am very particular about the way words are used. If words, especially technical or scientific terms, aren't used with precision, a potentially fruitful discussion can quickly collapse into a pointless argument. Consistent and clear definitions of key words are especially important in the context of controversy. Are we dealing with a controversial issue in this book? Clearly we are. I could argue passionately that it shouldn't be controversial, but the reality of its controversial nature, especially here in North America, cannot be denied.

So, let's aim to use key terms in a way that avoids confusion wherever we can. That may require us to be picky about precise definitions from time to time, but I'm convinced that verbal precision is essential to this topic. I've seen too many discussions about evolution end up in a muddle of misunderstanding because people failed either to define key terms carefully or to use them consistently.

Take the word *evolution*, for instance. I suspect that the first thing that comes to mind for most people is biological evolution, a package of explanatory theories that biologists have formulated to account for the way that life forms have changed on Earth over time. But the same word *evolution* is used by other scientists as well. Astronomers, for example, use the term *stellar evolution* when they talk about how stars are formed and change over time. Geologists and planetary scientists speak of *planetary evolution*— the formational history of planets such as Earth.

When our editor uses the term *theory of evolution,* he makes it clear that he includes not only biological evolution, but stellar evolution, planetary evolution and the evolutionary formation of other kinds of structures as well—the chemical elements, spacetime, galaxies and the like. Furthermore, questions of timescale—the age of the universe, the age of planet Earth—are also included in what the editor calls the *theory of evolution.*

There's nothing wrong with that, especially after all of the various parts of this broad theory have been put in place. But in order for me to explain how scientific evidence leads me to accept this all-inclusive theory of evolution, I find it necessary to examine that theory one component at a time. I believe this piece-by-piece approach will also help the reader to avoid a number of misunderstandings that still persist in the mind of the general public. I know that confusion and misunderstandings are out there. I've been an active participant in discussions on evolution and religion for more than a quarter of a century. That's why I am dividing our editor's inclusive question about the theory of evolution into a series of more restricted questions, some focused on timescales, and others on the formational histories of particular kinds of structures.

In the process of doing this, however, we will discover something very important about the set of answers that we obtain—their consistency, their harmonious relationship to one another. Even though each of the individual answers has its own integrity, we will find that they relate to one another in the same way as the voices of several instruments engaged in playing one grand symphony.

So, let the symphony of evolution begin.

A. What Is the Age of the Universe?

First, what exactly is the *universe*? It's just the whole shebang, right? The entire collection of planets, stars, galaxies, quasars and anything else that happens to exist out there in space? Well, not exactly.

Yes, all of the differing kinds of objects that I just listed are parts of the universe, but there's more to the universe than what appears on a list of components, just like there's more to an automobile than what appears on a parts list. The universe is also characterized by its *organization* and its *systematic behavior*.

Here's one way to build the idea of the universe as an integrated, functioning system. Thousands of years ago in Ancient Near Eastern culture, it was common to think of the world as divided into three distinctly differing regions: the Heavens, home to many of the more exalted gods; the earth, our home place; and the Underworld, home of the not-so-nice gods. I have sometimes called this kind of world a "triverse" because it was composed of *three* vastly differing regions and members.

Similarly, in Ancient Greek philosophy it was common to think of the world as divided into *two* contrasting regions: the Celestial Realm, the heavens, marked by constancy, perfection and eternality; and the Terrestrial Realm, our earthly world, marked by change, imperfection and temporality. You could call this concept a "biverse" because of its vision of a world made up of two very different regions occupied by two kinds of things and behaving according to two very different sets of patterns.

The world now known to the natural sciences, however, is properly called a "universe" because of the oneness or uniformity of its nature. Our physical/material world (everything that scientific instruments can detect) is made of the same kinds of ingredients everywhere, and the behavior of these ingredients conforms to the same general patterns (laws of nature) wherever and whenever we look.

Here's the central point: our universe is not just the list of substances and things we find in it. It is that *plus* the fact that these materials and structures function in a consistent manner at all times and places. Even more than that, our universe functions as an integrated system of interacting parts. Some parts of the universe are near, some are far away. Some are huge in size, some are small. Nevertheless, all of these parts work together to make the universe one system. Understanding the universe as an integrated system is very much like realizing that our bodies are made up of many different parts—cells, tissues and organs—but these many parts work together as one system.

So how old is the universe? How long has this integrated system, our universe, been in existence? People have wondered about this for a long time, but only during the past century has it become possible to compute reasonable answers based on observations and measurements.

Piecing together the what-happened-and-when story of the universe's formational history is one of the major accomplishments of twentieth century science. For most of the past century, astronomers and cosmologists—the people in the best position to judge—have been aware that the age of the universe is several billions of years. The ballpark figure I usually offered my students was fifteen billion years, give or take a couple of billion years.

How are such numbers computed? By many different means, each yielding essentially the same result. Let's look briefly at a few of them to illustrate the general methodology.

1. Computing the Age of the Universe from "Look-Back Time"

The distances to stars and galaxies can be measured in a variety of ways. Consulting a textbook in astronomy would provide several examples of the methods that astronomers employ. The results of these distance measurements can be expressed in familiar units like miles or kilometers. However, because the distances encountered in astronomy are so large, astronomers find it convenient to use larger distance-units. One of these larger units is the "light-year," defined to be the distance that light, traveling at its fixed speed of 186,000 miles per second, travels in one year. A distance of one light-year is roughly equivalent to six trillion miles.

When looking through astronomical telescopes, we realize that we are looking at objects very far away in space. But we must also understand that we are looking at events and processes that occurred far back in time. For example, if some star is 8,000 light years away from us, it took 8,000 years for light to travel from there to here. That means that the light now being received from that star was produced and sent on its way 8,000 years ago. So, the light now coming into our telescope is telling us what that star looked like and was doing *then*, not now. That unavoidable time delay is called the "look-back time" for that star.

Similarly, when we look at a galaxy a billion light-years away (which means that its look-back time is a billion years), we are seeing it as it was, doing what it was doing, a billion years ago. The most distant objects that astronomers have detected are located at distances in the ten–fourteen billion light-year range. From that observation we conclude that the age of the universe—the whole cosmic system of which we are a tiny part—is in the ballpark of fourteen billion years.

2. Computing the Age of the Universe from "Expansion Time"

A quite different way of computing the age of the universe is based on a feature of the universe that was discovered about three-quarters of a century ago: our universe is expanding. On average, galaxies are getting farther apart from one another. This is happening not because they are moving to new places in space, but because space itself is expanding. I know it's not easy to think about space as a kind of "something" that could expand, but that is the way cosmology understands the large-scale interaction of matter and space.

Now, because the universe has expanded to its present size, and because we can measure the rate at which it has done so, it is possible to compute how long it took the universe to reach its present state. This *expansion age* also turns out to be in the fourteen billion-year ballpark.

The most precise value of the expansion age of the universe is derived from measurements made by instruments in orbit around the earth. These measurements have provided a detailed mapping of the *cosmic microwave background radiation*—the cooled off remnant of radiation produced in the aftermath of the big bang with which our universe began. It turns out that the brightness of this radiation is not precisely the same from all directions. From measurements of the slight variations in this brightness, cosmologists have determined many properties of the universe, including its age, which is now computed to be 13.7 billion years.

3. Computing the Age of the Universe by Multiple Methods

Another method of estimating the age of the universe involves determining the ages of star "clusters" (swarms of stars that formed relatively close together and at approximately the same time) and inferring that the age of the universe cannot be less that the age of the oldest star cluster in it. The result: an age value for the universe in the same ballpark as that computed in the previous two techniques.

One especially noteworthy point is this: several different and independent methods of computing the age of the universe produce essentially the same result. There is no way to force the consistency of these results, nor would a scientist have any desire or motivation to do so. Nonetheless, each method of computing the age of the universe yields essentially the same value, with honest recognition of appropriate margins of uncertainty, of course. This agreement among values computed independently of one another is one of the primary reasons that scientists have confidence in the results. To use the metaphor we introduced earlier, the harmony we hear affirms that all instruments are playing the same symphony.

Another point worth noting here is that none of these methods for determining the age of the universe depends in any way on the concept of biological evolution. And saying that the universe is 13.7 billion years old does not say anything about the adequacy or inadequacy of the several theories that contribute to the concept of biological evolution. Nothing positive; nothing negative; just nothing. What it does contribute is a broad time limit for the duration of life. The phenomenon of life in this universe cannot be older than 13.7 billion years. Biology has no choice but to work within the time restriction imposed by cosmology.

B. What is the Age of Planet Earth?

Putting Earth in Its Place

Earth is one of several planets in orbit around the sun, which is a rather ordinary type of star, called a main sequence star (more about this term when we talk about the formation of stars). Earth is ninety-three million miles from the sun, a distance that light can travel in eight minutes. The system made up of our sun plus the planets as well as several smaller types of objects that also orbit the sun (comets, meteoroids, and asteroids) is called the solar system. Astronomers have long thought that many other stars are also accompanied by systems of orbiting planets. Recent observations confirm that this is the case.

The sun is only one of the hundreds of billions of stars that are members of the Milky Way Galaxy, a spiral-shaped collection of stars, star clusters and interstellar nebulae (glowing clouds of gas and dust that reside mostly in the spiral arms of our galaxy). Our Milky Way Galaxy is approximately 100,000 light years in diameter, a rather typical size for spiral galaxies. In the early 1900s it was believed that ours was the only galaxy in the universe, but subsequent observations have established that hundreds of billions of other galaxies are also members of the visible universe. Galaxies are usually spaced a few million light years from neighboring galaxies and can be seen at distances as great as ten–thirteen billion light-years.

Stars are formed when gravity induces the collapse of concentrated globules of gas and dust that are found within interstellar nebulae. Planets are now understood to be by-products of star birth. The globules that collapse to form stars generally have some rotational motion. When a rotating globule collapses, some material is usually left in orbit around the newborn star. Some of this material collects into smaller lumps, such as planets, that remain in orbit around the parent star. Our solar system was formed in this way in one of the spiral arms of the Milky Way Galaxy.

Earth's Age

Since the sun and planets formed at about the same time, what we call the "age of the earth" is essentially the age of the entire solar system. The numerical value of this age can be computed in a number of ways. One of the most fruitful methods involves the study of meteorites. *Meteoroids* are small objects that apparently solidified early in the formation of the solar system and remained in a variety of orbits around the sun. Occasionally a meteoroid will collide with the earth. Passing first through Earth's atmosphere, these high-speed pebbles and rocks glow brightly (and we then call them *meteors*) because their surfaces get very hot from friction with Earth's atmosphere. Some of these meteors manage to reach the earth's surface (when they do this we call them *meteorites*) and become available for scientific analysis, which often includes the computation of the meteorites' age.

Some of the elements in these samples of early solar system material are radioactive. The radioactive elements that are especially useful in this context are uranium, thorium, rubidium, potassium and samarium. Crystals of radioactive metals and minerals trap the products of their radioactive decay. By measuring the relative amounts of parent and daughter elements (the elements before and after radioactive decay took place) it is possible to compute the amount of time that has elapsed since the crystals first formed. Most meteorites have age values clustering around 4.6 billion years, which is reasonably interpreted to be the age of the Solar System.

Using similar techniques, we find that although the ages (amount of time elapsed since crystallization) of rocks on Earth do vary, the maximum is approximately 4 billion years (some zircon crystals appear to be even older, about 4.3 billion years). Mineral samples taken from the moon also have a variety of ages, the oldest being in the neighborhood of 4.5 billion years. So it seems quite evident that our solar system formed about 4.6 billion years ago, with the earth and moon forming very soon thereafter. In other words, the system of sun and planets is only about one-third as old as the universe as a whole.

Readers may also have heard of radiocarbon dating (or carbon-14 dating) as a method of determining the age of materials, but this method applies only to things that were once alive and it does not help in determining the ages of the solar system, the earth or the moon. Furthermore, radiocarbon dating is useful only in determining the amount of time that has elapsed since the death of organisms that died within the past 50,000 years or so.

Once again, it is important to note that none of these methods for determining the age of the solar system, earth or moon depends in any way on the concept of biological evolution. However, since life on Earth cannot be older than the earth upon which that life arose, biologists have little choice but to work within the time constraint imposed by Earth's age. The phenomenon of terrestrial life can be no older than approximately 4.5 billion years.

C. Reconstructing Formational Histories

People have long wondered about how the world originated. Early ponderings about such matters were usually set in the framework of *mythological* stories—not mythological in the trivial sense of being mere fiction, but mythological in the far more noble sense of being creatively crafted accounts that embodied a community's vision of a deep Sacred Mystery whose presence is experienced, but whose ultimate nature is more than words could ever capture.

When viewed through the reshaping lens of modern Western culture, some of these mythological stories have been misunderstood to be answers to today's scientific questions about what happened and when in the universe as we now know it. As a general rule, however, the idea that such knowledge was within human reach would have sounded foreign to ancient cultures. On the basis of the high achievements of several ancient cultures, I presume that these were intelligent and sensible people who knew the limits of their knowledge.

Today, however, we have a very different situation regarding the deep history of our universe. In the last couple of centuries the natural sciences have discovered that the formational history of the earth, of stars, of galaxies, and of the whole universe is something to which we have access by way of observation, measurement and disciplined theorizing. What we see and measure today reveals a great deal about what happened yesterday. The formational histories of things can now be reconstructed with considerable accuracy on the basis of observational evidence that is systematically interpreted by professional scientists. Here are a few samples of what we have learned.

A Brief History of the Universe.

When air is allowed to expand into a larger volume, its temperature will drop (unless, of course, heat is added). A similar cooling has occurred as a consequence of the expansion of the universe. This cooling was confirmed by the observation of the cosmic background radiation, first detected in 1965 by Arno Penzias and Robert Wilson. The microwave background radiation is the cooled off remnant of electromagnetic radiation generated during the early phases of the universe's hot big-bang beginning.

Theories that trace the formational history of the universe from its beginning have been formulated on the basis of all the physics we know, tested by comparison with all relevant observations, and refined as needed. The process is something like running a movie backwards. If the visible universe today is expanding and cooling, then yesterday (or a billion years ago, or ten billion years ago) it must have been hotter and more dense (the same amount of matter packed into a smaller volume). Running the movie backwards for 13.7 billion years brings us to t=0, time zero on the cosmic clock, the first moment of cosmic history as we are able to model it. What may have existed before that beginning is simply beyond our scientific reach.

At t=0 the universe was, in effect, in a state of practically infinite temperature and infinite density: everything was at one place, the only place that then existed. Moving forward in time from that beginning, expansion and cooling are persistent themes. As expansion proceeded and the temperature dropped, various kinds of fundamental particles were able to precipitate out of the superhot cosmic soup. Among the first particles were the quarks, soon followed by protons and neutrons, which are aggregates of three tightly bound quarks. Next there was a period during which some of these protons and neutrons combined to form small atomic nuclei, mostly helium. At the conclusion of this period, a few minutes after time zero, the ordinary matter component of the universe was about three-quarters hydrogen nuclei and one-quarter helium nuclei. It was still too hot, however, for these atomic nuclei to combine with electrons (also part of the mixture) to form ordinary atoms. That "recombination era" (actually representing the first combination of atomic nuclei and electrons) occurred about 400,000 years later when the temperature had cooled to about 3000 Kelvins (about 5000 degrees Fahrenheit). As a consequence of this transformation of nuclei and electrons into ordinary atoms, light (one form of electromagnetic radiation) could for the first time travel freely over long distances.

One of the consequences of the expansion of space is that the wavelength values of light traveling through it also get stretched. The cosmic background radiation that Penzias and Wilson discovered is the cooled off and stretched out remnant of the light released into a transparent universe at the recombination era 400,000 years after the beginning at t=0.

Galaxy and star formation began within the first billion years after t=0. Most galaxy formation was completed by t=2 billion years, but star formation within galaxies continues to this day.

The Formational History of the Sun and Other Stars.

What looks to the casual observer like the central star in the series of three spots of light that comprise the sword of Orion the Hunter, a familiar constellation seen in the northern hemisphere's winter sky, is actually not a single star but a magnificent interstellar nebula (glowing cloud of gas and dust) with more than a hundred stars embedded in it. Among the embedded stars are four especially bright ones, called the Trapezium, that provide most of the energy that makes the nebula glow. The Orion nebula is located at a distance of 1500 light-years from Earth, has dimensions in the neighborhood of thirty–forty light-years, and contains as much matter as thousands of suns.

The Orion Nebula is but one of thousands of "stellar maternity wards" associated with our Milky Way Galaxy. These nebulae are the sites of star birthing that is happening at this very moment. Star birthing begins when a protostellar globule (a more concentrated mass of gas and dust within the larger nebula) begins to collapse under its own weight. Gravitational collapse causes the material of the globule to heat up, the familiar consequence of compression. If the collapsing system is sufficiently massive, its central core will become hot enough (about ten million Kelvins) to ignite a process known as thermonuclear fusion, the same process that generates the explosive energy of a hydrogen bomb. Larger atomic nuclei are made by fusing smaller ones together, a process that generates huge amounts of energy.

Once the fusion process has begun, the gravitational collapse will be slowed down because the added heat produced by fusion tends to cause expansion. Eventually (typically a few tens of millions of years after the beginning of the collapse), the collapsed and fusion-powered object settles down to be a relatively stable and familiar object, a star. Not just any kind of star, but a particular variety called a main sequence star. Main sequence stars maintain their steady energy production by the fusion of hydrogen nuclei into helium nuclei, and they are approximately a million miles in diameter. The sun, for instance, is a main sequence star. Stars like the sun (that is, stars made of the same amount of material) stay in that stage for about ten billion years. At 4.6 billion years in age, the sun is a middle-aged main sequence star.

According to stellar evolution theories, the sun will come to the end of its main sequence lifetime about five billion years in the future and be transformed into something structurally quite different—a red giant star, hundreds of times larger that the present-day sun, similar to the star Betelgeuse in the constellation Orion. Some time later the red giant star will become unstable and shed its outer layers, leaving behind its small inner core, a white dwarf star (about the size of the earth, only 1 percent the diameter of the sun) that will eventually cool off because fusion is no longer taking place.

The three major types of stars—main sequence, red giant and white dwarf—were well known to astronomers before stellar evolution computations were available. What these quantitative theories contributed was the discovery that these star types were related to one another as sequential stages in the life history of stars. Theories built on the assumption that the formational history of stars can be understood as a natural process have been extremely fruitful in understanding why stars display the particular properties that we observe and measure.

As a general rule, it is difficult to determine the age of an individual star. However, clusters of stars formed from the same nebula within a relatively brief time interval do display a pattern of characteristics that allow astronomers to compute the amount of time that has elapsed since the cluster formed. Interestingly, the maximum age of clusters determined in this way turns out to be in the ballpark of ten–twelve billion years, just a bit less than the age of the universe reported earlier.

Note the consistent picture that is now emerging. The computed age of the universe is 13.7 billion years. Star clusters, which are components of galaxies, come in a variety of ages, but all less than about twelve billion years. The solar system, a product of the star formation process just outlined, is 4.6 billion years old. Theories of cosmic evolution, galactic evolution and stellar evolution—all based on the best physics we know— produce a consistent picture of natural formational processes. Consistency of this sort (or harmony, using our symphony metaphor again) is the hallmark of good science and rightly contributes to confidence in the theorizing process.

Finally, a familiar reminder: Nothing we have said so far depends in any way on the success or failure of theories of biological evolution.

An Overview of Earth History

Formed from a disk of material left in orbit around the just-formed sun, planet Earth's first few hundred million years of geological history were turbulent times by present-day standards. The earth's surface was bombarded with numerous meteors, large and small. Heat generated by meteor bombardment and several other processes led to the melting of a large fraction of earth material. The more dense metals sank to form the planet's molten metallic core. Less dense materials rose and collected at the surface, where they cooled and solidified to form the earth's early crust. Gases released from this process contributed to the earth's early atmosphere. Some gases escaped into space; additional gases were released from the earth's interior as a consequence of volcanic activity and contributed to our atmosphere over time. Compared to today's atmosphere, Earth's early atmosphere contained far less oxygen and far more carbon dioxide.

Within the first billion years of Earth history, oceans began to form from water vapor contributed by volcanoes and by comets entering Earth's atmosphere. Intense volcanic activity persisted until about 2.5 billion years ago and continues to this day, but at a lower rate. Some of the material ejected by volcanoes in the form of molten lava and ash landed in the oceans and sank. Additional contributions to sea-floor sediments came from the erosion of landmasses and were carried to the ocean by wind and rivers. Sedimentary layers that were formed at the bottoms of oceans, lakes and elsewhere are rich with information about Earth history. The goal of historical geology is to put together a what-happened-and-when story that accurately reflects Earth's formational history and helps us to account for the nature and appearance of Earth's surface today.

It is essential to keep in mind that the surface of the earth is continually in the process of change. This includes the locations of major landmasses and oceans. As one example of the remarkable changes that have taken place, consider what today's continents have done to get where they are now located. When we view the earth's surface at any one time, it seems quite solid and immovable; hence the common designation, "terra firma." However, suppose that we had a series of photos of Earth's surface taken once every 25,000 years and then arranged for each photo to serve as one frame of a movie shown at thirty frames per second. Five minutes of that movie would show what changes took place over a time span of about 225 million years.

If we were to watch that movie, what would be our impression of Earth's surface? Instead of looking like terra firma, it would look like several relatively flat chunks of solid material (called *tectonic plates*) floating on hot liquefied rock (a very viscous liquid, like thick molasses) and moving around in response to the flow of the liquid beneath them. Continents, which reside on many of these plates, move with the plates beneath them and go along for a free ride.

Tectonic plates move relative to one another, sometimes sliding past one another, sometimes colliding. The San Andreas Fault in California, for instance, represents the boundary between two plates sliding past one another. A large portion of California's west coast is sliding northward toward Alaska at an average rate of two inches per year. Oceans basins, such as the Atlantic, are formed when two plates move away from one another over extended periods of time. Most of the Atlantic Ocean was formed by such seafloor spreading over the last 100–150 million years.

When plates are involved in a direct collision, mountains may be formed by material pushed upward, perhaps as a consequence of a buckling or crumpling process, at or near the collision boundary. The Himalayan Mountains, for example, were formed as a consequence of the head-on collision of the northward moving Indian Plate with the Eurasian Plate. This particular collision began about fifty million years ago, with the major episodes of mountain building occurring during the past ten million years.

But this collision episode was a small part of a much larger drama. About 250 million years ago, the land masses that now make up the major continents were gathered into an enormous "supercontinent" called Pangea. Covering about a quarter of the earth's surface, Pangea included both the northern continental group (Laurasia) and what would become the southern continents (Gondwana).

The Pangea supercontinent broke up into several sections that are now well separated from one another. The North American continent drifted away from both Gondwana and Eurasia. Gondwana split into two major pieces, now known as South America and Africa. What is now India raced (at the speed of six inches per year) northward and collided with Eurasia. Australia separated from Antarctica. The Atlantic and Indian oceans filled the basins formed between continents.

Terra firma has been busy getting shaped up for its appearance today. Earth has a formational history, and geologists have successfully put together major portions of its fascinating what happened-and-when story.

Once again, none of what we have said about Earth's formational history has required any knowledge regarding biological evolution.

D. Life on Earth

A Succession of Life Forms in Time

So far our focus has been on the formational history of inanimate physical systems. Now we turn our attention to the history of life forms on Earth. The most basic observation we need to appreciate is that vastly differing forms of life have lived on Earth at different times. Without needing to say anything about how they might have come to be formed, here is a list of the approximate times at which various types of organisms first appeared on Earth. Some of these forms have disappeared completely; some categories of forms remain even though the particular species present now are quite different from earlier species in the same category.

How Long Ago	What New Forms Appeared
3500 million years ago	Prokaryotic (no nucleus) single-cell organisms
1500	Eukaryotic (with nucleus) single-cell organisms
1000	Multi-cellular organisms (e.g., worms, sponges)
545	Hard-bodied organisms
545-525	The "Cambrian explosion" of diversification
500	Vertebrates (e.g., fish)
520	First land animals (e.g., millipedes)
350	Amphibians, insects, ferns
300	Reptiles
230	Dinosaurs
200	Mammals
136	Kangaroos
65	Dinosaurs become extinct; mammals thrive
50	Monkeys
20	Chimpanzees and hominid line
3.5	*Australopithecus* Lucy walks the earth
1.6	*Homo erectus*
0.2	*Homo sapiens neanderthalensis*
0.05	*Homo sapiens sapiens* (modern humans)
0.006	Writing
0.0001	Automobiles
0.00004	Space travel

How Are These Life Forms Related?

Once we realize that different life forms appeared on Earth at different times, normal curiosity will prompt us to ask important questions about the relationships among these forms: How are the members of this historical succession of life forms related to one another? Did these various species come to be formed (by whatever means, natural or otherwise) independently of one another? Or, on the other hand, is it possible that species can change over time and that early species are the ancestors of later ones? If so, is it possible that all forms of life present today share a common ancestry?

During the century before the work of Charles Darwin, biologists gave respectful scientific consideration to theories based on the premise of the independent formation of fixed species, that is, species that did not change over time. One significant philosophical reason for taking this approach may have been that the fixity of species seemed to follow from Plato's concept of eternal and immutable Forms or Ideas. In the spirit of Plato's philosophy, terrestrial species could be considered to be imperfect actualizations of perfect Ideal Forms that were inherently unchangeable. A non-scientific remnant of this fixed-species concept continues to linger, especially in North America, and has become associated with the religious belief that the Bible authoritatively teaches the concept of special creation, the idea that each biological *species* (or perhaps some higher level of categorization) was individually formed by the biblical Creator.

Over the last 150 years, however, it has become evident to biologists that independent formation theories and special creation scenarios failed to provide a satisfactory way of understanding numerous relationships that were exhibited either by successive forms in time or by similar forms at any one time. In 1859, Darwin, standing in the tradition of many theologically trained persons who became dedicated students of natural history, proposed in *The Origin of Species* that the historical succession of life forms on Earth were related to one another as members of a continuous parent-offspring sequence. From this point of view, all life forms that exist at a given time share a common ancestry with one another, having all evolved from earlier forms. Although that suggestion itself was not new, Darwin's proposal of a cause-effect process involving only natural causes, without need for form-imposing supernatural interventions, was quite remarkable in its time. The heart of his proposal was that offspring were not necessarily identical to one another but rather exhibited an array of variations, some of which would give that organism an advantage in producing more offspring that survived in the long run.

Reasons for the variations that Darwin posited were later understood in terms of genetics. Biologists now know of numerous natural processes and events that introduce changes in the genome (genetic information bank) of offspring relative to their parents. The term *natural selection* has come to represent the idea that some of these variations give organisms a reproductive advantage relative to others. Lines that are more successful at producing another generation of offspring will continue. Less successful ones will eventually become extinct.

Natural selection among genetic variants introduces neither more nor less hardship in the life experience of any individual. Each organism is born, lives for a time and dies. I must confess that I have never understood why biological evolution is sometimes harshly characterized as being more "red in tooth and claw" than life without genetic variation or natural selection. In either case, organisms are born, reproduce with some measure of success, live out their lives, and die.

The Last of Our Smaller Questions

Finally, then, here is the last in our series of smaller questions that are part of our big question about the theory of evolution. Why do I find the concept of biological evolution credible? Why do I judge that later life forms evolved naturally from earlier life forms?

As will become evident in the remainder of this chapter, my personal answer to this question will not be based on the claim that I have the professional training that would be needed to evaluate in minute detail each of the numerous biological theories that pertain either to genetic variation or to differential reproduction (natural selection). Instead, I will emphasize my respect for the way the scientific community has developed a process for making sure that such evaluations are being done, a) by the people most qualified to do so, and b) in a manner that discourages the insertion of mischievous distortions by persons with ideological agendas. So, it's time now to reflect a bit on the scientific enterprise in general.

II. ON THE NATURE OF SCIENTIFIC THEORIZING

A. What the Natural Sciences Are Trying to Accomplish

Many people have attempted to define exactly what science is, and every definition, no matter how carefully crafted, is open to criticism for its failure to meet some philosophical criterion. I won't pretend to offer a definition that would satisfy the technical expectations of a philosopher of science. Instead, I'll just say a few things about how I have experienced the natural sciences as a participant in the larger scientific enterprise.

I would characterize natural science as a disciplined way of observing, describing and theorizing about the natural world. The natural world is the world of physical/material things large and small, near and far. It includes the large and distant world of galaxies, stars and planets. It includes the small world of molecules, atoms and sub-atomic particles. It includes the world of inanimate structures such as continents and sedimentary rock. It includes the world of living things that are part of today's ecosystem, and the world of organisms large and small that lived millions and billions of years ago.

The natural world is the world that I can see, hear, smell, taste and touch. It's the world that I can detect with the aid of all manner of measuring instruments that amplify and extend the range of the human

30

senses. And, given all the information that has been gathered by our senses and scientific instruments, I can construct useful descriptions of what that world is like—its properties; its capabilities for acting and interacting; its behavioral patterns; the ways that its behavior is related to its properties; its remarkable capabilities for organizing into functional systems; and much, much more. While these descriptions may be incomplete and less than 100 percent accurate, they are nonetheless valuable as the starting point for our scientific theorizing.

The broad goal of scientific theorizing is to construct systems of thought that help us make sense of what we now observe or know. Some theories provide us with a means of connecting natural causes with observable effects. Others help us to understand how things got to be the way they are now as the outcome of natural processes. Contrary to the reckless anti-science rhetoric sometimes voiced these days, scientific theories are not mere guesses or wild fantasies. The construction of scientific theories is a creative but rigorously disciplined endeavor to portray realistically and accurately what the universe is and what it does. While the sciences themselves have no vested interest in serving the agendas of comprehensive philosophical, social, political or religious worldviews, some individuals and institutions representing broader worldviews do sometimes attempt to hijack science and to distort its agenda by forcing it into the service of warranting some particular tenet of metaphysics or religion. Such attempts should be, and are, vigorously resisted by professional scientists. When I characterize science as a disciplined way of going about its activities, I have in mind a style of thinking and acting that is characterized by methodical observation and measurement, by systematic organization and reasoned analysis of the results of these observations, and by the creative formulation and synthesis of theories (more on the nature of scientific theories to come) that give a satisfying account of how some particular kind of material, structure, system or organism now functions or how it got to be the way it now is.

B. What the Natural Sciences Assume

Assumptions about Our Observations of the Universe

The process of scientific theorizing must begin with some basic assumptions about the world that it studies. Many of these are best described as common sense assumptions that serve well to describe what we have learned from ordinary human experience. While they may be philosophically unsophisticated, they work. Here are some examples of

what I have in mind:
- The natural world actually exists. It is not merely a product of our mental activity. For instance, we assume that the moon is in orbit around the Earth whether we are looking at it, thinking about it, or sound asleep.
- Our minds are naturally inclined to craft stories about the character of that world. These stories are incomplete and vary widely in accuracy. Data for these stories come from diverse sources: observation, education, tradition, culture, fears, desires and the like.
- The goal of the natural sciences is to craft theories—disciplined stories—that are rooted in careful observation and accurate measurement.
- We (mind and body) interact with that world, each having some measure of influence on the other.
- Our senses (and instrumental extensions of our senses) give us empirical access to that world.
- Our senses are generally trustworthy within limits that can be openly investigated.
- Observational aids (such as telescopes and microscopes) and measuring instruments (such as thermometers and rulers) are trustworthy within limits that can be investigated.
- Our minds are capable of rational reflection on what our senses, observational tools and measuring instruments indicate to us.

Assumptions about the Nature of the Universe

We have already called attention to the idea that we are members of a universe, a harmoniously integrated system of interactive parts. In addition to what we noted earlier, the natural sciences also assume that:
- Our universe is everywhere made of the same basic kinds of raw materials. What are these raw materials? A physicist would probably focus on the various forms of energy and the most basic units of ordinary matter of which composite structures are made. Quarks, for example, are the elementary particles of which protons and neutrons are made. And light consists of a stream of photons, the basic units of electromagnetic energy. A chemist might focus on atoms and the structured combinations of atoms called molecules. From these raw materials a nearly infinite variety of functional material systems can be made, including living organisms.
- The raw materials of the universe and all objects made of these raw materials, behave according to the same patterns everywhere and at all times. In other words, the laws of nature are the same

both everywhere and "every-when."

- Natural phenomena have natural causes. Proceeding from this assumption has enabled scientists to discover a growing list of natural causes that allow them to understand the phenomena they observe. Because of the success of this natural causation principle, scientists are no longer inclined to posit the existence or action of non-natural agents to explain what takes place. Take the orbital motion of a planet around a star, for example. Understanding that this motion is caused by the natural action of gravity means that there is no need to posit that it is caused by invisible, unembodied spirits that steer planets in precisely ellipse-shaped orbits.

- The formational history of the universe is the outcome of natural phenomena, even if the very existence and the particular nature of the universe cannot be accounted for in terms of natural causes. That means that the natural sciences have every right to posit answers to questions such as: How did the solar system form by natural causes from an interstellar nebula? There are, of course, interesting and profound questions that fall outside of the domain of the natural sciences. These questions will have to be dealt with in some other way, or left to Mystery. Questions falling outside of the domain of science's competence include these: Why does any universe exist in the first place? Why is there something rather than nothing? Why does the something (this universe) that does exist have the particular nature that it does? Why isn't it an entirely different kind of universe?

The Right Stuff Universe Principle

It fascinates me to reflect on the most basic assumptions and principles that characterize the scientific profession. One that I find especially important and worthy of special attention here is the one I have named the "Right Stuff Universe Principle." I know that this terminology might sound a bit eccentric (you won't find it in the professional science literature) but let me explain briefly what I mean here by the "stuff" of the universe and what it takes for this stuff to be "right."

First, recall what we have said about the raw materials of which the physical/material universe is made. A feature that makes these materials especially interesting is that they are not inert but active. The raw materials of our universe possess a diversity of remarkable capabilities to act and to interact with one another.

Next, focus on the formational capabilities of these materials and of things made of these materials—their capabilities to act and interact in such a way as to form some new structure. Atoms, for example, have the capability to interact and to form a nearly infinite variety of molecules. On the larger scale, interstellar nebulae have the ability to act and interact in ways that lead to the formation of stars and planets. Living organisms have the ability not only to develop in time as individuals but also to give rise to generation after generation of offspring. The range of formational capabilities is astounding and this fact must not go unappreciated.

Finally, let me call attention to a feature of the universe that often goes unrecognized, but is nonetheless something that I consider to be indispensable: the necessity for the universe to possess a rich array of structural and functional potentialities. To grasp this concept, begin with this question: What must the universe possess in order that such functional structures as molecules, planets, stars, bacteria, sharks, orangutans and robins could form naturally?

One obvious part of the answer is that the universe must possess the requisite raw materials of which these interesting inanimate structures and living organisms are made. Fair enough, we've already taken note of that.

What else must be present for these structures and organisms to form naturally? Clearly, the raw materials of the universe must possess the requisite formational capabilities to assemble these functional structures and living organisms from their composite parts. We've already taken note of that also.

Is still more needed beyond the requisite raw materials and their formational capabilities? Yes, indeed. In order for raw materials to actualize a star, for example, what we call a star—everything that a star is and everything that a star does—must be a possibility. There must be the structural potentiality for heated spherical masses of hydrogen and helium to be held together by gravity and there must be the functional potentiality for that structure to generate energy by thermonuclear fusion so that a star will remain luminous for billions of years. The potential (the possibility) for the structure and function of stars must be written into the very fabric of the universe. If no potentiality for stars, then no stars, period.

And that consideration applies not only to stars, but to all functional structures, large or small, inanimate or living, that we might wish to name: atoms, molecules, planets, stars, bacteria, sharks, orangutans, robins and myriad other possibilities. These potentialities are an essential part of what the universe is. The very nature of our universe must include these potentialities. In fact, I am inclined to see these potentialities as far more interesting than just the raw materials of which things are made. In the course of time, some of these potential structures come to be actualized; that is, potential structures become actual structures. When the circumstances are right, the universe's raw materials use their formational capabilities to form a vast diversity of functional structures. Potentialities are transformed into actualities. Molecules form from atoms, stars form from interstellar nebulae, and offspring are produced by parents.

Now it's time to put this collection of ideas together. Think of all of these raw materials, all of their formational capabilities, and all of the structural and functional potentialities that have ever contributed to the formational history of the universe. Call this collection of materials, capabilities and potentialities the universe's "stuff." I sometimes refer to this *stuff* by the more formal name, the formational economy of the universe. By either name, however, it is the totality of all of the universe's resources, capabilities and potentialities that have ever contributed to the forming of new structures in the course of time.

Using this terminology, there are several ways to state a fundamental question about the nature of the universe. Stated informally, it reads, Does the universe have "the right stuff" to make possible the forming of every kind of natural structure (things not humanly fabricated) by natural means alone? Stated more formally: Is the formational economy of the universe sufficiently robust to make possible, without needing to be supplemented by any non-natural intervention, the formation of every kind of physical structure and every kind of living organism that has ever existed?

A couple of centuries ago, it was still common, even in scientifically active Western culture, to presume that the answer was, "No, natural causes are inadequate and must be supplemented by the non-natural action of some supernatural Agent." Now, however, having gained a greater appreciation of the richness (or robustness) of the universe's formational economy, the natural sciences make the reasonable assumption that our universe is a "right stuff universe." We assume that the formational economy of the universe is sufficiently robust to make possible the evolution, by the action of natural causes alone, of every kind of physical structure and every kind of living organism that has been a member of this universe. This is what I call the "Right Stuff Universe Principle" (RSUP).

I have put the RSUP in the category of assumptions because (like any other principle or theory in the natural sciences) it cannot be proved in the narrow logical sense. Nonetheless, it must be seen as a useful and productive working principle that has grown out of the total experience of the scientific community. Far from being a mere guess or a wild conjecture, the Right Stuff Universe Principle represents the collective judgment of the scientific community and is rooted in centuries of scientific experience and evaluation. It is held not because it favors any particular worldview, but because it works. Scientists are highly pragmatic individuals. If a principle works well for them, they stick with it.

The Art and Skill of Theory Formulation

Having characterized natural science as a disciplined way of observing, describing and theorizing about the natural world, we now focus our attention on the process of formulating and evaluating scientific theories. The process ordinarily begins with some combination of curiosity and observations. This, in turn, often leads scientists to posit better questions and to initiate a program of disciplined observations and measurements. But the results of observation and measurement cry out for some kind of explanation. Why, for example, are planets observed to orbit the sun in ellipse-shaped orbits? Why is the sun's surface so hot? Why does ice float on water? Why do the genes of humans so closely resemble the genes of chimpanzees? How can the particular results of observations and measurements best be explained?

The job of scientific theories is to provide the explanations that science seeks. As scientists go about their business of formulating theories, certain patterns of theorizing have become recognized as fruitful pathways toward understanding. I won't call them "rules" because there is no ruling body to legislate or enforce them. These patterns are just habits of the scientific community that have demonstrated their usefulness over the centuries.

Scientific theorizing is a form of "disciplined creativity." Human creativity is essential to the scientific enterprise, but the application of that creativity to the challenge of theory formulation must be constrained by the exercise of a form of self-discipline. Good scientific theories should, for example, be formulated in a way that makes them vulnerable to falsification (the process by which a theory could be shown to be incorrect) by comparison with observation. Scientific theories should be formulated in a way that clearly identifies the "mechanism" at work, that is, the chain of cause and effect that leads to some observed outcome. Furthermore, scientific theories formulated to give an account for what is observed should be constrained to posit only natural causes, that is, causal factors that are themselves a part of our universe. Theorizing in the natural sciences rightly refrains from positing non-natural, extra-natural or supernatural causes. When scientists fail to find a suitable natural cause, the most appropriate thing for them to say is simply, "I don't (yet) know what is causing X to happen." That's the spirit of the Right Stuff Universe Principle.

The Qualities of Good Scientific Theories

For any given set of observations, a scientist could propose a large number of explanatory theories. So how does the scientific community judge which is the "best" one? In the course of their work over the centuries, natural scientists have developed criteria that have served them well for evaluating theories. In general, a good scientific theory is one that:

• makes specific predictions that can be tested by comparison with observation

• where appropriate, makes quantitative predictions that turn out to be accurate

• does not contradict itself in any way

• is consistent with other relevant theories that have already proved useful in explaining observations and measurements

• applies to a broad category of similar natural systems

• unifies several categories of natural phenomena into a single comprehensive system

• is fruitful in stimulating a continuing program of research

III. WHY I BELIEVE IN THE THEORY OF EVOLUTION

First, recall that what our editor calls the theory of evolution is actually a collection of several theories, each focused on the formational history of some particular type of structure or system. Some of these theories are focused on cosmology, the formational history of the matter and space of the universe as a whole. Some deal with the manner in which particular kinds of astronomical structures—planets, stars, or galaxies—form and develop over time. Some are focused on the evolution of life forms on planet Earth after it became hospitable for the development of life.

As a matter of fact, I find each of these theories to be informative and worthy of respect, with the usual understanding that many interesting puzzles and details remain to be worked out. There is no reason to pretend that we know everything about how various structures or organisms evolved. But neither is there any good reason to treat today's incomplete or tentative evolutionary theories with disrespect, as if they were little more than guesses that can be glibly discarded for reasons of preference based on non-scientific concerns. Each of them has been formulated and evaluated by a community well known for its competence, discipline and professional integrity, the same community that has given us the knowledge that has been successfully applied to modern medicine, planetary exploration and the electronic gadgetry that we employ daily.

As I here briefly summarize my evaluation of current theories on cosmic, stellar, planetary and biological evolution, let me begin with a reminder. In this context, the word *evolution* means neither more nor less than the formation of various structures and systems (space, matter, galaxies, stars, planets, life forms) by the action of natural causes adequate for the task. Note well that this does not provide answers to questions such as these:

- Why is there any universe at all?
- Why does the universe have these particular natural capabilities?
- Does the existence and nature of this universe depend in any way on the action or will of a Creator?
- Is the existence and nature of this universe the expression of any purpose?
- What is the source of human moral awareness?

These and many other fundamental questions will have to be answered by means beyond the scope of science's evolutionary theories. Science is equipped to answer some kinds of questions well, others not at all.

Cosmic Evolution

Our awareness that the universe is expanding is relatively new. It is based on observational data collected early in the twentieth century. These observations led cosmologists to the conclusion (surprising to many at the time) that throughout the universe, galaxies are, on average, getting farther apart from one another. Recent evidence reveals that this cosmic expansion is no longer slowing down in response to the gravitational attraction between neighboring galaxies, but is now accelerating in response to a repulsive force arising from the presence of something (not yet well understood) known as "dark energy."

Theories to account for the universe's expansion in terms of particular features of the universe's nature have been around for decades. Their details are continually subject to modification in response to new observational data. I have no doubt that there will be additional adjustments to theories of cosmic evolution in the future. Nonetheless, certain broad features of today's picture appear to be quite stable and not likely to undergo radical change:

- Our universe began with a big bang—rapid expansion from an astoundingly dense and hot state.
- The cosmic microwave background radiation that we observe today is the cooled off remnant of that big bang beginning.
- The detailed nature of that radiation provides valuable

information about the nature of the universe, especially in its early stages.

- This beginning of our expanding universe can be dated to approximately fourteen billion years ago.
- Most galaxies in our universe formed before the universe was two billion years old.
- Star formation has occurred in our Milky Way Galaxy as well as other galaxies for more than twelve billion years.

Scientific theories of cosmic evolution that are constructed on the premise of the Right Stuff Universe Principle have been and will, I believe, continue to be remarkably successful. The success of these theories serves to build our confidence in the assumption that our universe is equipped with all of the physical resources, all of the formational capabilities, and all of the structural and functional potentialities to make cosmic evolution possible. The universe of today is intimately related to the universe as it existed at t=0. From the beginning until now, the universe's raw materials have employed their formational capabilities to transform potentialities into actualities.

Stellar Evolution

Similar statements can be made about our understanding of stellar evolution. Large interstellar clouds of gas and dust are found in the spiral arms of the Milky Way and other galaxies. Conditions and events within these nebulae trigger the collapse of compact globules of gas into newborn stars, often accompanied by disks of matter that provide the raw material from which orbiting planets are formed. Numerous star-forming regions have been observed. Representatives of stars at all stages of their developmental history have been observed. Star clusters, the systems of stars whose age can be most easily determined, have ages up to twelve billion years. Some stars expel their outer layers as spherical shells of gas late in their lifetimes. Numerous examples of such shells can be seen through modern telescopes. Some more massive stars become unstable and explode at the end of their lifetimes. These are observed as supernovas in the Milky Way and other galaxies.

Many more details could be added, but the bottom line is this: theories of stellar evolution that have been constructed on the basis of the Right Stuff Universe Principle have been remarkably successful in making sense of all of our observations of the properties of both stars and star-forming regions. The success of these theories serves to build our confidence in the assumption that our universe is equipped with all of the physical resources, all of the formational capabilities, and all of the potentialities to make stellar evolution possible. The formational history of stars is the consequence of natural processes that are open to scientific examination.

Planetary Evolution

Similar statements can be made about the formational history of the earth. Theorizing in historical geology is built on the premise that all earth-shaping processes and events are the consequence of natural processes that can be modeled after processes and events that are taking place here and now. Other scenarios have been tried, but they failed to give adequate explanations of what was actually observed. For example, a couple of centuries ago it was assumed that major features of the earth's present appearance were shaped by a cataclysmic global flood that took place within human history. But flood geology — the attempt to explain Earth's geological features as a consequence of this posited flood — failed. It failed not because of any ideological bias against it, but because it could not give an adequate account of what has actually been observed and measured. Theories of Earth's formational history constructed on the foundation of the Right Stuff Universe Principle have clearly demonstrated their superiority. The success of these theories increases our confidence in the underlying principles on which they are built. The earth of today is connected to the earth of 4.6 billion years ago through a continuous history of natural geological processes.

Biological Evolution

Like the theories of cosmic evolution, stellar evolution and planetary evolution to which we have referred, scientific theories of biological evolution are also constructed on the premise of the Right Stuff Universe Principle. Given the high degree of success experienced in cosmology, astronomy and geology, I believe that we are fully warranted in expecting that natural causes will be found sufficient for biology as well, and that there is no need for them to be supplemented by non-natural (supernatural) interventions.

For this reason, I believe that biologists are on solid ground in constructing explanatory theories based on the premise that the historical succession of life forms that have crawled, flown, floated, swum, walked, slithered or rooted within Earth's biosphere are related to one another as parent and offspring. Assuming the applicability of this common ancestry thesis has made theorizing about life's formational history remarkably fruitful, certainly more fruitful than any approach based on the Platonic concept of fixed species. The track record of evolutionary theorizing continues to reinforce our confidence in the soundness of the approach. Theories of biological evolution have become indispensable in our scientific effort to make sense of what has been observed in disciplines ranging from paleontology to genetics.

Theories describing the formational history of the chemical elements can be constructed in considerable detail and subjected to many kinds of observational tests. That's because the structures and processes involved are relatively simple and amenable to mathematical modeling. Likewise, constructing theories regarding the manner in which stars form and develop with time is relatively straightforward. Comparing the predictions of these stellar evolution theories with the observed nature of stars, including some rather dramatic events such as supernova explosions and the formation of neutron stars (stars made up mostly of neutrons), provides strong affirmation that our computational models are right on track.

As a consequence of the inherent complexity of organisms relative to atoms or stars, modeling the evolution of life forms cannot always be done to the same level of detail as modeling the evolution of the chemical elements or of stars. Although many processes and events directly relevant to biological evolution can be described in detail and tested by observation and experiment, others cannot. When detailed step-by-step reconstructions of evolutionary histories are not yet possible, the best available theories may temporarily take the form of plausibility arguments that demonstrate the high likelihood of some posited scenario.

Some persons have used the employment of such plausibility arguments as an occasion to cast a broad shadow of doubt on evolutionary theorizing in biology. I find no scientific merit in that rhetorical strategy. Given the success of theorizing based on the Right Stuff Universe Principle in the arenas of cosmology, astronomy and geology, I see no warrant whatsoever for questioning the use of the same foundational principle in the arena of biology.

Stated more positively, given the fruitfulness of the Right Stuff Universe Principle in biological theorizing generally, and in certain portions of evolutionary theorizing specifically, I feel fully justified in accepting it as the guiding principle for scientific theorizing about the overall formational history of life on planet Earth. In my mind, the phenomenon of biological evolution is just as firmly grounded on sound principles and is just as positively affirmed by empirical evidence as are the phenomena of cosmic evolution, stellar evolution or planetary evolution.

We do indeed live as members of a cosmos—a harmoniously integrated universe equipped with a robust formational economy that has made possible the awe-inspiring drama of its evolution from a hot big bang beginning to the wealth of structures, systems and living organisms we see today. From the opening clash of cymbals until now, many instruments have joined in playing one symphony.

Let There Be Light!
By Rabbi David E. Kay

A sectarian[1] once came to Rabbi Akiva and asked him, "Who created this world?" Rabbi Akiva replied: "The Holy One, Who is blessed." So the sectarian said, "Show me a clear proof." Rabbi Akiva replied, "Come back to me tomorrow."

On the next day the sectarian returned and Rabbi Akiva asked him, "What are you wearing?" The man replied, "A garment." Rabbi Akiva asked him, "Who made the garment?" The man replied, "A weaver." Rabbi Akiva answered, "I don't believe you. Show me a clear proof."

The sectarian replied, "What can I show you? Don't you know that a weaver made it?" Rabbi Akiva answered, "And you— don't you know that the Holy One, Who is blessed, created his world?

When that sectarian departed, Rabbi Akiva's students asked him, "What's the clear proof?" He answered them, "My sons, just as a house indicates that there's a builder, and a garment indicates that there's a weaver, and a door that there's a carpenter—so the world indicates that there is a Creator: the Holy One, Who is blessed."

—MidrashTemurah

Some 1,500 years before René Descartes offered a logical proof of the existence of God in the third of his *Meditations on the First Philosophy*, Rabbi Akiva offered this simple and elegant argument. As with Aristotle's idea of a universal "prime mover," Rabbi Akiva understands that the intricate and harmonious workings of the natural world must have some sort of underlying organizing principle.

This isn't necessarily such an obvious conclusion for Rabbi Akiva. His world is very complex and even more chaotic. He lives in first-century Judea, in the midst of the same general political and cultural upheaval which gives rise to the roots of Christianity. Rome rules the region with an iron fist, and thousands of Jews are put to death. A sense of

---

[1] Hebrew, *min*, from the root meaning "type" or "kind." During the period of Greek and Roman rule of Judea, there were several sects [1]of Judaism, some of which the ancient Rabbis considered outside of the norm. In Rabbinic literature, a *min* often appears as a skeptic whose ulterior motive of discrediting one of the Sages of the Talmud is thwarted by the Sage's wisdom.

desperation fills the community, and would-be messiahs spring up, their followers grasping at the shreds of miraculous hope they offer. Even the wise and learned Akiva falls under the spell of one of them, and as a result ends up being tortured to death by the Romans.

Akiva was a man of great faith and towering religious learning. But he was also schooled in both the linear logic of Greek philosophy and the more subtle construction of Talmudic argumentation. Through this balance, Akiva and his peers recognized what our most advanced science now confirms: even that which appears most random actually has a fundamental order to it.

In attempting to understand the universe at this most basic level, scientists have delved much more deeply than we can ever actually see. We were all taught in school that an atom is the basic unit of matter. But the atom itself is made up of protons, neutrons, and electrons. And if an atom is made up of these smaller particles, it seems logical to assume that *those* particles are made up of even smaller units. Where, we may certainly ask, does it all end (or begin)?

It was Albert Einstein who theorized the general answer to this quest for the ultimate structure of the universe: everything is actually made up of energy. Energy can't be created or destroyed, according to our understanding, only transformed. Sometimes energy is put to work, and sometimes it's stored up, often in the form of matter. For example, a piece of wood might not seem like a storehouse for energy, but set it on fire, and it will release much of that energy as heat and light.

But what is energy made of?

At the most basic level, we understand energy as different sorts of *fields*, regions of space characterized by a physical property. Some of these, such as electricity and magnetism, we know to actually be different expressions of the same field. The great disappointment of Einstein's life was that he could never demonstrate that what he knew intuitively must be true: *all* energy fields are actually different expressions of the same fundamental and universal energy.

In working with Einstein's theories over the last century, physicists have come to the remarkable conclusion that there really could be fundamental units of existence that are orderly in ways beyond ordinary understanding. Here science and religion blur and merge. Like Rabbi Akiva, physicists rely on the observable and measurable effects of the fundamental units as evidence that they exist, even though they cannot actually be seen or measured themselves.

The genius of Rabbi Akiva's "proof" of God's existence is not so much in the elegance of his argument as it is his turning the tables on the questioner. This is not merely a "gotcha," though. As clever as it is, Akiva's answer to the sectarian makes a fundamental point about the intersection of science and religion: both, to one degree or another, are a matter of faith.

The sectarian's question is more than a request for information. The Hebrew word translated as "sectarian" suggests that this person is deliberately trying to bait or embarrass Akiva. Rather than engage Akiva in a direct and respectful discussion of ideas, the sectarian poses an impossible challenge: give me tangible proof of your intangible God.

Akiva's response is precisely appropriate. The sectarian's demand for proof is a logical impossibility. By asking the man to come back the next day, Akiva can now confront him with the same sort of flawed demand. By reversing the roles, the sectarian *must now answer his own question*.

The primary argument invoked by persons of faith who see the theory of evolution as conflicting with religious doctrine or belief is that there is no "clear proof" that evolution "works." If what is meant by "clear proof" is really *"direct* proof," then—like the sectarian's—the demand is fatally flawed. Our response should therefore be, like Akiva, to turn the question around and ask for clear proof (that is, *direct* proof) that Darwin got it wrong.

Of course, there is evidence which points to problems, inconsistencies, and alternate explanations in Darwin's original theories and the refinements and expansions that have come from them in the intervening century and a half. That's to be expected.

No theory is considered plausible in science unless it can, in principle, be refuted.

That's worth repeating: no theory is considered plausible in science unless it can be refuted. At first glance, this idea seems crazy: in order for a theory to be taken seriously, it must be possible to argue that it *shouldn't* be! But what this really means is that true science doesn't claim to have the final answer to anything. It recognizes what every faith tradition teaches: human beings aren't perfect. As amazing as the human intellect might be, it's no match for the vastness of the entire universe.

So what does a scientist like Darwin mean when he says "I have a theory"? He means that he has observed a particular phenomenon that intrigues him. In looking for an explanation, he has made many observations, gathered information, analyzed it, formulated possible reasons, tested them, rejected the ones that don't fit, made projections based on the remaining possible reasons, tested those, and rejected the projections that don't work.

A theory, then, isn't simply a scientific opinion. Nor is it necessarily the most likely sounding explanation for something. Theories stand on their own, anchored in observations and data compiled over a period of time. And they are constantly being refined.

Darwin's theory of evolution is no different. In the interest of fairness, we need to pause here and admit that Darwin explicitly rejects Rabbi Akiva's proof of the existence of a Creator. As a student at Cambridge University in England, Darwin learned and accepted William Paley's "Argument from Design," essentially, a scientific presentation of the same idea put forward by Aristotle, Akiva, and Descartes. However, once he refined the idea he would call *natural selection*, Darwin came to believe that the perfection of design and adaptation in species came from a process that takes place within nature rather than supernaturally.

The concept of natural selection, a core concept in the theory of evolution, is perhaps the single most misunderstood and misrepresented scientific idea ever. The underlying principle in natural selection is "survival of the fittest." This is also the underlying source of all the misunderstanding and misrepresentation. "Fitness," in the evolutionary sense, has a very specific meaning.

To be evolutionarily "fit" means *to pass one's genes to the next generation*. The more effective and efficient an individual is at this, the better that individual's evolutionary fitness. Being larger, stronger, faster, or even smarter can sometimes help, but none of these attributes is a guarantee. In fact, they may turn out to be no advantage at all, in the evolutionary sense, if they don't help the individual produce offspring.

The Hebrew Bible records a classic case of misunderstanding this principle of evolutionary fitness. Concerned that the captive population of Israelites in Egypt is becoming too large, Pharaoh decrees that all newborn Israelite boys be killed, but the girls be left alive.

If Pharaoh had understood population dynamics, he would have seen the folly in this decree right away. Since polygamy was permitted in ancient Israelite culture, reducing the number of new *males* in the population would have barely cut into the population growth at all. With the female population unaffected, the potential number of pregnancies in the next generation would be exactly the same.

In fact, in evolutionary terms, then, Pharaoh only succeeded in *increasing* the fitness of males who had already been born. Let me explain.

Let's suppose there were 500,000 adult Israelites of reproductive age at the time Pharaoh made his decree to kill all newborn male Israelite children. About half of those (250,000) would be males and half (250,000) females. That's a 1:1 ratio of potential fathers to potential mothers. To make things easier, we'll assume that each of these 250,000 pairs of potential parents produces one child during the year following Pharaoh's decree. That's 250,000 new babies, half of which (125,000) are boys and the other half (125,000) are girls.

If Pharaoh's cruel orders were carried out on all the baby boys, there would be 125,000 new females and no new males added to the population. Eventually, these baby girls grow up and become of age to marry. By that time, about half of the original 500,000 adults would be too old to reproduce. That leaves 125,000 males and 125,000 females as potential parents from the original 250,000 of each. Now we add the 125,000 new adult females and we have a total of 375,000 adult Israelites of reproductive age: 125,000 males and 250,000 females.

The ratio of males to females is 1:2, meaning that the potential for any particular male to pass his genes on to the next generation is now *twice* what it was before Pharaoh's orders were carried out.

This dramatic increase in evolutionary fitness among Israelite males had absolutely nothing to do with their strength, speed, skills, or intelligence. The only qualification they share for this incredible benefit is that each was already born.

Many people of faith would say that this was entirely a matter of chance, that by being in the right place (already alive) at the right time (a tragic moment when those males not yet born would be killed at birth), they were given an advantage they neither expected nor planned for. Others would suggest that the inclusion of this story in the Bible is evidence enough that it was *not* a matter of chance, but rather part of the divine plan. Indeed, all three of the faith traditions represented in this book, my own and that of my Christian and Muslim co-authors, include a version of this story in their sacred texts. From the purely literary perspective, we can understand Pharaoh as the embodiment of human corruptibility, and the redemption of the Israelites as the paradigm for God's protection and love of justice. That Pharaoh's nefarious scheme to curtail the population growth of the Israelites was at best ineffective (and at worst achieved the opposite) fits this model of deliberate divine planning exactly.

Yet these two approaches to the same text aren't contradictory. In fact, they are simply different facets of the same jewel. At no time does Darwin's model rule out the possibility, or even the necessity, of a divine Creator. It doesn't *assume* the existence of God, but (despite the way it has been portrayed over the years) it doesn't *deny* it, either. Like all good scientists, Darwin doesn't submit his ideas as a challenge or alternative to God, but rather as another context in which human beings might understand a complex and elegant part of the natural world.

As an illustration, let's use a contemporary example of Rabbi Akiva's logic, applying it to that most necessary of modern necessities, the automobile. Let's say you live in San Diego, and your car was manufactured in Detroit. If a neighbor in San Diego demanded "clear proof" as to who (or, in these days of computerized manufacturing, *what*) assembled your car, you could not provide it. The brand plate, vehicle identification number, and various stickers are evidence, but you couldn't introduce your questioner to a specific person or machine. Yet the very existence of your car would demonstrate that *someone* (or *something*) had assembled it.

Now let's take it a step further.

When your car is parked, or idling at a stoplight, or even zipping down the highway, you can't show any "clear proof" *why* it moves. Again, there's ample evidence to support your claim that it is the engine that's responsible—you can turn it on, hear it run, show receipts for fuel. But, once again, it's the fact that it *is* moving that demonstrates that something must be *making* it move. Really, if you want to understand cars, you have to understand how the engine works. After all, that's the whole point of the automobile: to move! The question of *who* (or *what*) made the car (or the engine) isn't important now. It's a given that it exists: we want to know how an *existing* mechanism works.

In order for us to understand evolution on its own terms, then, we can subscribe to whatever answer to the question, "How did everything come to be?" that we choose. To really understand what evolution is and how it works, we need to know what makes it go. "Survival of the fittest" is only the fuel on which the engine of evolution runs. The engine itself is natural selection.

Where Did the Grackles Go?
A Personal Encounter with Natural Selection

When I was a child, growing up in Chicago, there were large populations of grackles living in my neighborhood. Grackles are birds that have very little going for them, really. They aren't especially attractive (even their name is unflattering), and they have raspy, raucous voices. The last thing you want to wake up to in the morning is a flock of grackles calling.

When I went off to college, the grackles were still the most noticeable species of bird in my otherwise quiet residential neighborhood. As I made my home elsewhere—first at college and then in a series of apartments—my trips to my parents' home in my old neighborhood were more spread out. After a few years, I began to notice something strange: the grackles were all but gone, but a larger and larger number of crows— bigger, even less attractive, and even more annoyingly raucous—were in evidence.

Where did the grackles go? I wondered.

Fortunately, my parents had paid good money for me to get an undergraduate degree from the Department of Ecology, Ethology, and Evolution at the University of Illinois, and I was particularly qualified (or had better be) to look for an answer to this mystery.

First of all, I had the *empirical* evidence at hand. *Empirical* evidence or data is that which can be directly observed. This is what you might call "raw" data or information. So far, the empirical evidence was limited to two events: (1) grackles, which had formerly been present in large numbers, were now rarely, if ever, seen; (2) crows, which had formerly rarely, if ever, been seen, were now present in large numbers.

It seemed likely that these two events were somehow related, but so far I had no evidence or theory to support that assumption. What I did have was a limited number of possible explanations for the disappearance of the grackles: (1) they left; (2) they died; or (3) they were driven away. In order for this event to be linked to the simultaneous appearance of the crows, I now had three possible and complementary explanations: (1) they filled the vacancy left by the departing grackles; (2) they filled the vacancy left when the grackles died, which might include being responsible for their deaths; or (3) they filled the vacancy left when the grackles were driven away, which might include being responsible for driving them away.

There were no reports of large numbers of grackle carcasses being found, so it didn't seem like disease or violence was doing them in. While crows are significantly larger than grackles—a common grackle is about a foot from beak-tip to tail-tip, while an American crow may be six inches longer—they don't eat grackles or grackle young. The eastern grey squirrel will eat grackle eggs, but the squirrels and grackles had co-existed in my neighborhood for decades.

It could be, I postulated, that a few crows had found their way into the area and colonized it. Both species nest in trees and are more or less omnivorous, that is, they will eat almost anything from insects to seeds to leftovers in people's garbage. Being bigger and heavier and therefore needing to eat more and have larger nests, the crows may have simply out-competed the grackles for food and nesting spaces.

But in order for that to work, food and nesting resources had to be insufficient to support *both* species, and that just didn't seem to be true. What's more, there didn't seem to be much overlap between the decline of the grackle population and the increase of the crow population. If the crows had moved in on the grackles and forced them out, you would expect to begin with a large number of grackles and a small number of crows, then see the grackles gradually disappear while the crows became more numerous. Instead, what I observed was that the grackle population seemed to have declined noticeably *before* the crows showed up in any significant numbers.

Only one of my three original explanations could now make it all fit: the grackles left, and the crows colonized the vacancy in the neighborhood ecosystem. But that left me with an important question still unanswered: *why* did the grackles leave? If they weren't driven out, why did they abandon a habitat where they had lived and bred happily for many generations?

The most likely answer seemed to be a change in the habitat, which now made it unsuitable (or, at least, much less suitable). The air quality, water quality, and available grackle-food quality was no better or worse in my neighborhood than in other areas of Chicago where grackles were still found in the same numbers. A somewhat sleepy collection of bungalows, my old neighborhood had seen no new development, no major construction, no parks replaced by high-rises or four-lane thoroughfares. In fact, very little had changed.

Except for the trees.

My old neighborhood was originally laid out by a developer who only got as far as building a few white-stone, three-story apartment buildings and planting "skyline" elms in all the parkways along what were supposed to be the side streets before he was wiped out in the 1929 stock market crash. Twenty years later, my parents picked out a one-quarter-acre plot of mud where their house was to be built in the revived project, which had been incorporated into the southwest edge of the city of Chicago. Each new house had the added bonus of now-mature elm, whose branches stretched far enough to meet those of the trees across the street. The resulting canopy of leaves and branches provided a high, shady roof under which we played endless games of baseball every summer of my childhood.

But in the mid-1960s, Dutch elm disease began to take these majestic trees. First as single isolated incidents, then in clusters, and later along entire blocks, the old elms would wither and die. That leafy canopy became patchy then disappeared. The elm in front of my parents' house was one of the last to succumb.

The city of Chicago takes its official motto, *Urbs in horto* (A City in a Park), very seriously. No sooner did an elm come down than a new, but obviously smaller and younger, tree was planted in its place. Homeowners had a choice of a few hardy types, bred specifically to flourish in urban and suburban settings. Young and sapling locusts and maples now lined my old street.

The decline of the grackles, I realized, roughly paralleled the loss of the elms. The appearance and increase in the population of crows roughly paralleled the rate of the replacement of the dead elms with other species of trees.

Now the puzzle seemed complete. I theorized that the grackles had been nesting in elms for some forty years by the time Dutch elm disease started ravaging the trees. As the elms began to disappear, the grackles went farther afield, looking for the familiar trees. Eventually, there were no elms left, and no grackles either. By the time the elms had all been replaced, the grackles had already gone away, looking for greener pastures.

Meanwhile, a few crows, some of whom might have been there or nearby all along, showed up. As newcomers, they wouldn't have any attachment to elms as nesting sites. Thus, as the new trees were planted and grew for a few years, there were more and more places for the crows to live.

Assuming this model is correct, we can see how the engine of natural selection, fueled by the concept of evolutionary fitness, drove the replacement of grackles by crows. The grackles couldn't adapt to the change in local habitat (the loss of the elms), and were no longer able to produce offspring there. Failing to effectively pass their genes on to the next generation (that is, being evolutionarily unfit) meant that the local population of grackles would quickly die out. However, those grackles who could adapt, either by selecting other nesting sites or seeking another area where suitable nesting sites were available, *would* successfully reproduce.

That's exactly what natural selection means: when there is a change in the ecosystem, those individuals who carry the ability to adapt to the new set of circumstances will still be fit (reproduce). As long as their offspring carry the same adaptation and the ecosystem remains stable in its new form, the descendants of those individuals will flourish. By contrast, those individuals who cannot adapt to the initial change will be less likely to reproduce, and their genetic material will quickly disappear from the population.

Black Moths and Better Monkeys

Of course, the most famous demonstration of the principle of natural selection is the English peppered moth. As the name suggests, this is a light-colored moth with black speckled wings. Its coloring is perfectly adapted to resting on the trunks of lichen covered trees. The moth blends in with this pale mottled background so well that it is very difficult to see.

This strategy, found in many species, is known as *protective coloration*. Blending in almost invisibly as it rests on a tree means that the English peppered moth is less likely to be seen—and eaten—by a hungry bird. First and foremost, "survival of the fittest" requires just plain survival. If you get eaten before you reproduce, the likelihood of passing your genes on to the next generation is zero. Thus, natural selection would favor the genes for peppered coloration. Genes for coloration patterns that don't afford protection from predators would be removed from the population.

But every once in a while a completely black-pigmented English peppered moth would still pop up. This *melanistic* type was quite easy to spot against the pale speckled background of a lichen-covered tree trunk. Being a melanistic peppered moth meant losing all the advantage of your species' protective coloration, essentially ringing the dinner bell for local birds.

Melanism in the English peppered moth is the result of a *recessive* genetic trait. As its name suggests, a recessive gene can be carried and passed from generation to generation without being expressed. But occasionally—and usually when the same recessive gene is passed to an offspring from both parents—it does express.

Expression of some recessive genes doesn't seem to matter much, or doesn't have any particular positive or negative effect. Others are clearly harmful. Still others, as with the melanistic peppered moth, aren't fatal in and of themselves, but may create a disadvantage in a particular environment.

But if there is a change in the environment, a genetic trait that has previously had no particular value or has even been undesirable can suddenly create a tremendous advantage. If the neutral or negative trait allows the individual to adapt to the environmental change, it will most likely increase that individual's evolutionary fitness. At the same time, if the genetic traits of the *status quo* in the population aren't helpful in adapting to the environmental change, those individuals *without* the formerly neutral or negative trait will become *less* fit.

In the late 1800s, the Industrial Revolution led to dramatic increases in the use of coal to run the new factories springing up all over England. In heavily industrial areas, coal soot covered the trunks of trees, killing the lichens and changing the surface color from pale and speckled to almost entirely black. Suddenly, the "normal" protective coloration of the peppered moth made it stand out against the dark tree trunk like chalk on a blackboard. It was a feast for the local birds.

Meanwhile, the rare melanistic moth actually benefited from the loss of the lichens and the build-up of soot. The all-black insects were now virtually invisible, and in areas of heavy industrial pollution, melanistic moths rapidly became the common form.

Had things continued unchanged, the recessive melanism gene would probably have become "fixed" and the peppered pattern all but disappeared in moths living in those areas.

Before that could happen, though, the human population decided it didn't want to keep breathing such badly polluted air. New technology and tighter controls on emissions from the factories reduced the amount of soot and improved air quality. The lichens started to grow again, and the peppered coloration regained its protective value. Melanistic moths were once again at a disadvantage. Their numbers decreased and the peppered pattern made a dramatic comeback.

The important point in both the rise and fall of the melanistic moth population and the case of the disappearing grackles is that what works for a population in one set of circumstances doesn't necessarily work when the circumstances change. This is a powerful logical argument for a natural mechanism by which species retain a whole lot of variation, even when those variations don't provide any immediate benefit. And, sometimes, even when they pose something of a problem.

Sickle cell anemia is a serious genetic illness that disproportionately affects persons whose ancestors come from certain areas of the world, particularly Africa. When a person has sickle cell anemia, the hemoglobin—the oxygen-carrying protein—in his or her red blood cells tends to "collapse" when it releases its oxygen, causing the usually doughnut-shaped cell to flatten into the telltale crescent shape that gives the disease its name. These cells get caught in narrow areas and smaller vessels in the circulatory system, causing pain and potentially fatal obstructions, among other problems.

Genes come in pairs, one version received from each parent. If a person gets the recessive sickle cell hemoglobin gene from both parents (recessive *homozygote*), he or she will have the full blown disease. But if a person gets the sickle cell gene from one parent and the normal hemoglobin gene from the other (*heterozygote*), he or she will have *sickle cell trait*. In this case, some of the red blood cells will have sickling hemoglobin, but the rest will be normal. Under most circumstances, a person with sickle cell trait will not experience any severe symptoms.

Now let's look at the sickle cell phenomenon in terms of natural selection. If we turn back the clock just one hundred years or so, to a time when sickle cell disease was poorly understood, treatment options were severely limited, and mortality very high, we can say with confidence that a person with full-blown sickle cell disease would not be evolutionarily fit; that is, he or she would be much less likely to pass his or her genes on to the next generation.

But what about the person with sickle cell trait? Except in certain cases where the person is stressed by lack of oxygen—for example, at high altitude—his or her condition would have little or no impact. Being a *heterozygote*, having one normal hemoglobin gene from one parent and one sickle-cell gene from the other, doesn't seem to significantly affect this person's evolutionary fitness either way.

However, it's long been known that the sickle cell hemoglobin gene is found primarily in populations living in regions of the world where malaria is widespread. Malaria is caused by the microorganism, *Plasmodium sp*, whose spores are carried in the gut of the female anopheles mosquito and injected into the bloodstream when she bites.

The spores are carried to the liver, where they continue their life cycle, eventually spreading to the red blood cells, where the parasite feeds on oxygen-carrying hemoglobin.

Having a percentage, but not all of one's red blood cells containing sickle cell hemoglobin actually provides some defense, by making those cells inhospitable to the plasmodium parasite. In malaria-stricken areas of the world, then, sickle cell trait—being a heterozygote—makes you more likely to survive a bout of malaria. By contrast, individuals who are *homozygotes* and have normal hemoglobin will have a higher mortality rate for malaria than those who are heterozygotes.

Let's call the normal hemoglobin gene "H", and the recessive sickle cell hemoglobin gene "h." When two heterozygotes (Hh = sickle cell trait, which provides some defense against malaria) produce children, on average one in four (25 percent) will receive the "H" gene from both parents and have all normal red blood cells, but also be more likely to die from malaria. One in four (25 percent) will receive the "h" gene from both parents, and will likely die of sickle cell disease before reproducing. But two of four (50 percent) will receive an "H" gene from one parent and an "h" gene from the other, and will be heterozygotes, like their parents.

At one point long ago, the sickle cell hemoglobin gene was a *mutation*, a change in the building blocks of a particular gene. In areas of the world where malaria is rare or unknown, this mutation would be completely deleterious, meaning that it is not only of no benefit, it is actually undesirable and life-threatening. However, when it occurs in a malaria-stricken part of the world, the deleterious nature of the homozygote is far outweighed by the benefit of the heterozygote. Natural selection not only keeps the mutation in the population, it ensures that a large part of the population will carry it.

Notice that, in the case of the English peppered moth, the species didn't *become* black in order to adapt to the change in the color of the tree trunks. Likewise, here in our example of the sickle cell hemoglobin gene, the mutation for this gene didn't occur in *response* to malaria. In both cases, a gene that had no benefit or was actually deleterious turns out to be advantageous in adapting to an environmental pressure.

Natural selection is an *adaptive* process, not a creative process.

The theory of evolution does not say that one species somehow actively "improves" itself to become a new species, either by chance or by choice. Rather, it explains the value of maintaining a wide variety of species, as well as why closely related or similar looking species appear in many different forms in different environments.

Evolution doesn't claim that species, including our own, got to where they are by a series of random events. Rather, it gives us a plausible method by which those species could persist, flourish, and diversify over time.

A common misstatement about human evolution is that it professes that human beings, through a series of happenstance, developed from monkeys over a period of hundreds of thousands of years. The converse of this wildly inaccurate declaration would be that evolution teaches that today's monkeys will eventually evolve into humans.

Neither of these statements in any way reflects the reality of evolutionary theory. First of all, if there are no changes in climate, habitat, environment, predation, disease, etc., the engine of natural selection would be expected to remain in neutral, or at the very least in low gear. "Living fossils" like the American alligator, for example, have remained mostly unchanged for eons. Superbly adapted to their surroundings for millennia, alligators experienced very few mutations that produced traits to improve on that adaptation. If evolution really meant that species inevitably morphed into new species over time—and particularly ones that were more human-like—alligators would have long since started wearing boots instead of being turned into them.

Evolution, therefore, does not predict that monkeys will eventually become humans. Evolution predicts that monkeys will become better monkeys.

By "better" we mean better adapted and more evolutionarily fit. Some adaptations selected for by evolution, such as melanism in the English peppered moth, are visible ones. Others, such as the sickle-cell hemoglobin gene, can't be seen with the naked eye. In technical terms, evolution works at the level of *genotype* (genetic characteristics) rather than *phenotype* (the physical expression of genes). In fact, some changes in genotype which make an individual more evolutionarily fit may not be measurable at all.

The expression of genes that influence behavior doesn't show up in the physical appearance of the species (as they did in the peppered moth) and can't be seen under a microscope (as can that of the sickle-cell gene). For example, many species exhibit genetically coded *courtship behavior* as part of their reproductive cycle. Obviously, the more adept an individual is at courtship behavior, the more likely that individual will be to pass genes on to the next generation.

A bird with a genetic make-up that produces, let's say, a song that is more attractive to potential mates will not have any measurable difference in appearance or physiology from others of its species, yet it is clearly more fit than others of its kind. This bird will be much more likely to reproduce, and do so more often, and those of its offspring whose genetic make-up produce the "improved" song will do likewise. As generations pass, the "improved" song can be expected to become more and more common in the population, probably even replacing the original song.

But now that the "improved" song has become the standard, there is no longer any special advantage of fitness in having it. This will be the *status quo* until a new mutation produces an even more attractive song, or perhaps "improves" on another element of courtship behavior. So what about those dramatic changes in the structure and appearance of species which are so commonly associated with the process of evolution? Does evolution really hold that new species arise from previously existing species? Indeed it does. Changes in morphology and *speciation*—the emergence of discrete new species of plants or animals—are also an important part of evolutionary theory.

The Neck of the Giraffe

Several years ago, my family and I had the opportunity to spend a few days in the Transvaal of South Africa, staying in a small villa in the midst of a game park. One afternoon, a giraffe literally appeared out of nowhere. It was impossible to believe that anything that large and that tall could have come into the resort area unnoticed. But there it was, almost as if it had materialized behind the villas. It's one thing to see a giraffe in a zoo or even from a jeep during an early-morning game drive. It's quite another to crane your neck in order to watch one contentedly munching leaves from the lowest branches of a thirty-foot acacia tree.

The neck of the giraffe has long been the subject of discussion among both theologians and biologists. "What was God thinking?" the theologian might ask, which is essentially the same question as the biologist's: "What's the advantage to the giraffe in having a body like that?"

The layperson's answer to the biologist's question is often, "To reach food on higher branches." With our understanding of how evolution really works, we now know that reaching food indeed is an *advantage* of the giraffe's body, and particularly of that incredible neck. But we also understand that the giraffe did not deliberately evolve a long neck for the *purpose* of reaching higher branches.

Evolution postulates an earlier form of what became the giraffe we know, one that may have had a similar body type, but a much shorter neck. A modern relative of our familiar gentle giant that looks very much that way is the *okapi* or *forest giraffe*. Like any species, our prehistoric "proto-giraffe" population contained individuals that all looked basically the same, with a narrow range of differences in size, weight and proportions.

We can't know for sure what pressures in that primordial

environment were responsible, but somehow, those proto-giraffes with longer necks developed an advantage in evolutionary fitness. A logical guess would be that their longer necks helped them compete better for food. That might have been because the ground plants and smaller trees were being overgrazed, or because taller species of trees had out-competed shorter species, or new animal species were moving in and depleting the proto-giraffe food supply. Whatever the reason, longer-necked proto-giraffes ate better, stayed healthier, lived longer and reproduced more.

Now, we can imagine this process continuing gradually, with natural selection working towards longer and longer necks, along with the internal changes in muscles and circulatory system that would make a much longer neck workable. At some point, giraffes would have long enough necks to reduce the food-competition pressure to a low enough level that further lengthening wouldn't provide them any particular advantage.

If, indeed, that's the way the giraffe evolved, then we'd expect to find skeletons of many *intermediate forms* between the okapi-like proto-giraffe and the long-neck wonder we know today. Using carbon dating and other techniques, we would expect that the oldest forms would have the shortest necks, and that neck length would gradually increase in the progressively younger specimens.

The problem is, it doesn't seem to work that way at all.

So far, anyway, there don't appear to be a number of intermediate forms with gradually longer necks. Instead, there are sudden jumps in morphology, and then large gaps of time until another change shows up. This has led skeptics to suggest that evolution as Darwin envisioned it doesn't happen at all, and that evolutionary biologists are lining up the skeletons of similar-looking creatures in chronological order in an attempt to force the evidence to fit the theory.

We can't over-emphasize the seriousness of such a charge. It would be the worst kind of bad science, something to which Darwin himself would surely object. Let us remember that Darwin learned, taught, and originally subscribed to the "Argument from Design." His theory of evolution and its engine of natural selection came *after* careful and thoughtful observations. Darwin, like all good scientists, did not start out with an idea and then begin looking for evidence to support it. Rather, he observed a phenomenon, an apparent "glitch" that didn't fit the accepted scientific theory and recurred repeatedly over time, and he sought a scientifically sound explanation for it.

The Problem of "Intermediate Forms"

So how can we clear this hurdle of the apparent dearth of intermediate forms in the fossil record? Did Darwin have a good idea, but ultimately get it wrong? The most intense scrutiny of his work consistently says "No." We may not find the number of intermediate forms that Darwin's theories seem to predict, but that doesn't mean we throw the theoretical baby out with the statistical bath water.

It was Mark Twain who observed the problem with statistical predictions. "There are lies," he is quoted as saying, "damned lies . . . and statistics." Just because a theory or statistical analysis predicts a particular outcome, event, or the like, it is rarely 100 percent (another statistic!) reliable.

Let me offer one last personal example:

I currently live in central Florida. During the rainy season, local weather forecasts talk about percent *rain coverage*. Growing up in Chicago, it was always the percent *chance of rain*. In the temperate Midwest, the weather service could estimate how likely it was to rain *at all* that day. A 20 percent chance of rain meant that, in all likelihood, it would be dry all across the metropolitan area. Whether you went to the beaches on Lake Michigan or Brookfield Zoo, fifteen miles inland in the western suburbs, you had an equal chance of sunshine.

By contrast, a 20 percent *rain coverage* in Orlando means that it's going to rain somewhere, the question being, will where you are (or want to be) that day be part of the 20 percent at the time you're there.

It's the same 20 percent chance of getting rained on, the same raw statistical datum. Yet, they mean very different things.

Similarly, when my family and I first moved to Orlando, there hadn't been a hurricane strike in more than twenty years. Being inland of both the Atlantic and Gulf coasts, Orlando wasn't as vulnerable as the cities right on the shore. The chance that we would experience a hurricane in our first year in town was so small as to be statistically insignificant.

Within six weeks, we rode out not one, not two, but *three* hurricanes — an experience less likely than hitting the lottery jackpot or being struck by lightning.

What this all comes to teach us is that, while Darwin's theory does, in a sense, anyway, *predict* the existence of intermediate forms, it does not require them. Like the subtle but highly significant difference between a 20 percent chance of rain and a 20 percent rain coverage, we can understand Darwin's prediction from more than one perspective. The fact that intermediate forms are not easy to find for *all* species (the "rain chance" model) doesn't negate the fact that intermediate forms appear very clearly and elegantly for *some* species (the "rain coverage" model).

There are, in fact, very reasonable explanations for "missing links" in the evolutionary chain of many species. Some of these we've already discussed: important adaptations that improve evolutionary fitness may have to do with things like behavior, coloration, the function of internal organ systems or hormonal systems, ability to resist disease, and other vital elements which would not show up as changes in the fossilized remains of an animal.

Second, in expecting a series of intermediate forms which show very gradual changes over time, we are forgetting that quick and dramatic changes in environment may make neutral or even deleterious mutations suddenly extremely adaptable. Since these mutations would appear in extremely low numbers in the overall population, we would not expect to find them until *after* they became advantageous.

To return to the example of the giraffe's neck, let's suppose that among the okapi-like proto-giraffes, there was a rare and recessive "long-neck" gene. Once in a blue moon, a long-neck proto-giraffe would be born. It would be at no particular disadvantage in obtaining food, but its appearance may make it less likely to mate. Scattered over the many square miles that these prehistoric proto-giraffes inhabited and over many generations, there might be the remains of several dozen long-neck types, and hundreds of thousands of normal-neck types. The chance (statistics one more time!) of finding the fossilized remains of a long-neck is virtually nil.

Now let's suppose that there is a sudden change in the environment, perhaps a rapid climate change such as drought, or the intrusion of a new species of leaf-eating ground animal, or an outbreak of a fatal parasitic plant disease. Whatever it is, let's imagine it decimates the population of smaller trees. Larger trees, perhaps because they are resistant to drought or parasites, or already too tall to be eaten by the intruding species, survive. There's only one problem for the proto-giraffes: the surviving trees are just a bit too tall for them to reach the leaves.

But not for the rare long-neck type of proto-giraffe. It can reach the lowest branches easily. Now, the statistically insignificant percentage of long-necks survives while the "normal" proto-giraffes slowly starve; an abundant source of food just inches out of their reach. Within a generation or two, "normal" proto-giraffes would be all but gone. It would take several more generations to build up the long-neck types into large enough numbers that their remains could be found by us, hundreds of thousands of years later. As a result the fossil record would look like this: there were normal-neck proto-giraffes, which disappeared; there was a gap of many years, and then long-neck proto-giraffes appeared. No intermediate forms can be found.

And yet, natural selection and evolution have worked perfectly in this scenario.

Finally, there is a very simple and very humbling explanation for the problem of intermediate forms, one that every person of faith should find completely satisfactory: human beings are imperfect, and we don't know everything.

You see, one compelling reason why we haven't found intermediate forms for every species, in addition to all the reasons given above, may well be that we just haven't found them yet. Considering the billions upon billions of creatures that have lived and died on and under the earth, and in the vastness of its rivers, lakes, and oceans, we have uncovered only the tiniest fraction of their remains. Many of those remains we will not and cannot ever find. The forces of nature have transformed them completely into earth, rock, minerals, even the fossil fuels we use to run our cars and power our homes. Like Rabbi Akiva, we can see the hand of the Creator in the creation, and still rest assured that rational scientific explanation of the elegance with which Creation operates reinforces our faith, rather than challenging it.

Scientific Theories of the Origin of the Universe and Life
By T.O. Shanavas

Science has become the engine of progress and for some the ultimate panacea for every human need. Even those religious people who deny the credibility of the most successful theories of science cannot live without the fruits of science in their daily life. Many Muslims, Jews and Christians feel threatened by the scientific theories of the origin of the universe and the human species. So, in any theological discussion it is essential to include a brief review of science, its methodology, and its theories that could impact Scriptural stories of creation.

Science and Its Methodology

Science is the systematic human effort to understand the way the natural world is structured and functions. Scientific methodology and logic are the appropriate tools for such a search. Scientists freely accept that these tools are not perfect. At the same time, scientists believe that repeated testing and experimentation ultimately lead to more and more confidence in the understanding of the material world.

Scientific theories are not immutable. The willingness on the part of scientists to modify their established conclusions is one of their greatest strengths when more or better data confront them. So, commenting on the ongoing debate between evolutionists, people who believe that the universe is about fourteen to twenty billion years old, and creationists, who believe that the universe is no more than 10,000 years old, anthropologist Ashley Montagu humbly admits, "Science has proof [for its theories] without any certainty [of new theories replacing the currently confirmed theories]. Creationists have certainty [of their creation stories] without any [experimental] proof."[1] Therefore, the contemporary theories and conclusions about any natural phenomena, including the origin and evolution of the universe and life in it, are uncertain truths even though they are based on repeated experiments and observations. Let us explore the current "uncertain" truths of science about the universe and life.

Cosmic Evolution: The Birth of the Universe

In past centuries, people believed that the stars were merely luminous objects affixed to the solid sphere of the sky. In 1718, when Edmund Halley noted that three of the brightest stars had changed their positions relative to the remaining stars, Western scientists realized that stars are moving objects. Then, in 1927, Georges Lemaitre claimed that the universe had an instantaneous beginning.

With the passage of time and the advancement of science, human understanding about their universe has changed. Human methods and tools used to understand and explain that universe have also changed remarkably. Physicists and astronomers now believe that insight into the structure of the atom will provide answers to inquiries regarding the nature of the cosmic egg and the origin of the universe. Individual atoms have a longer history than that of the earth because they are the elements from which the earth is made. Before atoms came together to form the sun and its planets, they were drifting in interstellar clouds. Therefore, we can come to understand the genesis and evolution of the universe by deepening our understanding of atomic and subatomic particles. The more we learn about the history of our universe, the closer we get to discovering the secret of its origin.

Protons and neutrons, the elementary particles of the nucleus, are made out of older particles known as *quarks*. We can learn more about protons and neutrons by accelerating them and allowing them to collide in a magnetic field, which reveals a wide variety of these older particles. Subatomic particles interact with the aid of four fundamental forces: gravitational force (gravity), electromagnetism, the strong force, and the weak force. Physicists believe that these four forces, in conjunction with atomic particles, generate every event in the universe. Gravitational force keeps the physical components of the universe together by mutual attraction. A particle known as a *graviton* is believed to carry the gravitational force between two material particles. Since the graviton has no mass of its own, the force it carries is long range. The gravitational force between stars and planets is attributed to the exchange of gravitons between the particles that make up these bodies.

Particles called *photons* carry the electromagnetic force by which electrically charged particles interact. Electric charges are of two kinds: positive and negative. The force between two charges is attractive when one is positive and the other is negative. The electromagnetic attraction between negatively charged electrons and positively charged protons in the nucleus causes the electrons to circulate around the nucleus of the atom.

When an electron in an atom jumps from a higher-energy outer orbit to one of lower energy that is closer to the nucleus, the energy difference appears in the form of a photon, which we see as light. The atom cannot exist without the strong nuclear force, which bonds the quarks when they form protons and neutrons and holds protons and neutrons together in the nucleus. This force is carried by another particle called a *gluon*, which interacts only with other gluons or with quarks. Finally, the weak nuclear force, carried by a particle known as a *boson*, helps the neutrons inside the nucleus to decay. The strong and weak nuclear forces operate only within the limited space inside the nuclei of atoms, while the range for electromagnetism and the gravitational force is infinite.

Physicists believe that when the big bang, the colossal expansion of space at the beginning of the universe, occurred, all four forces— gravitational, electromagnetic, strong and weak—were united under the extremely high temperatures of that time. The details of this process remain a mystery because no laboratory on earth can produce such temperatures. Only the high ambient temperatures at the genesis of the universe were hot enough to create and sustain such unity. The universe then started to expand and cool. Gravitation became a distinct force 10^{-43} seconds later. Further cooling to about 10^{-27} degrees centigrade at 10^{-35} seconds after the big bang allowed the strong force to become distinct. After about 10^{-10} seconds, electromagnetism and the weak force emerged.

Therefore, the universe began from an extremely hot dense state (about 10,000 billion degrees centigrade) after the primordial explosion called the big bang. The reason for the explosion and the source of the entity that exploded remain a mystery, but what is clear is that all matter and energy now in the universe was at one point of time condensed into a single point, sometimes called a "cosmic egg," at an extremely high density.

Physics does not have any explanation for the beginning or creation of the universe, when everything in the universe was condensed to a singularity in which the density of matter was almost infinite in value and space-time was reduced to a mathematical point. In this singularity, the extreme heat unified all four forces.

Similarly, the origin of the four fundamental forces and quarks remains a mystery. Are the four fundamental forces really fundamental? Is the quark a final elemental particle that is itself indivisible? Nevertheless, after the colossal explosion called the big bang, the universe began an expansion that has never stopped.

The evidence for the expansion of the universe originally came from a study of the variation in the frequency of sound originating from a moving train. In 1842 Christian Doppler pointed out that the frequency of the sound we hear is higher when a train is approaching and lower when it is moving away. This is known as the Doppler Effect. The French physicist Armand Fizeau showed that the Doppler Effect applies to light as well. The light frequency is lower when the source of light moves away from the observer and higher when it approaches. When light passes through a spectroscope, light waves spread out. The lowest frequency visible wave (red) will be at one end, and the highest frequency wave (violet) at the other end. Light waves between the red and violet waves correspond to various frequencies. As a result, we get the following order of color: red, orange, yellow, green, blue, and violet. Where some of these wavelengths are missing, we see dark lines on the spectrum. When a star moves away from Earth, the dark lines shift toward the red end of the spectrum. This is called *red shift*. If the star gets closer to the observer, the dark lines shift to the violet end of the spectrum. The observation that dark lines shift towards the red end of the spectrum led Edwin Hubble in 1929 to the conclusion that different galaxies (collections of stars) are moving away from each other and that the universe is therefore expanding.

While the big bang theory has convinced many scientists that it accurately describes the creation and evolution of the universe, there have been competing cosmological theories that also attempt to explain cosmic origins. In the steady state theory of Fred Hoyle, Thomas Gold, and Hermann Bondi, there is no big bang; new matter continuously appears in an expanding universe. In the cyclic model, the universe has existed eternally but has undergone repeated series of explosions and implosions. Nevertheless, the scientific evidence favors the big bang theory and a very old universe. In the west, mainly in the United States, some members of the religious right passionately argue for a less than ten thousand-year-old baby universe. So, how old is the universe?

The Age of the Universe

According to scientific calculations, the universe began expanding about fourteen to twenty billion years ago. However, there are many people, for example, some Christian literalists, who believe in a very young six-thousand-year-old universe. There is, however, much evidence against this scenario. For example, observance of a cross section of a tree shows an annual variation in its growth that is indicated by a series of concentric rings, one for each year of growth. The number of rings in the cross section is equal to the age of the tree. The oldest known trees are the bristlecone pines. A study of these pines and their concentric rings shows that some of these trees are approximately eight thousand years old.

Another argument against belief in a recent origin of the universe involves the observation of the speed of the travel of light. The speed of light is 186,000 miles per second. The distance that light travels in a year is called a light-year. It takes about eight minutes for light to reach Earth after it leaves the sun. The spaceship *Voyager*'s signals from Saturn reached Earth more than an hour and a half after they were transmitted. Many of the stars we see today are millions of light years away. This means that we see them as they were millions of years ago, when their light left them to travel toward us. Therefore, we must concede that these stars are several million years old, which makes a few-thousand-year old universe unacceptable.

Yet another argument against this belief involves continental drift, which is the large-scale horizontal displacement of continents relative to each other. At one time, all the continents were a single landmass. The continents that made up that landmass gradually drifted away from each other. The motion of the continents can be measured by laser satellite experiments. These experiments show that the continent that contains America and the continent that contains Europe are separating at about two centimeters per year. At that rate, the twenty-five-hundred-mile separation between the Atlantic coastal lines of America and Europe required a period of approximately 200 million years to take place. Therefore, the earth must be at least 200 million years old. Now that we have gained insight about the universe's past, we are in position to consider how it may evolve in the future.

The Future of the Universe

Most astronomers agree on how the universe evolved after the big bang. Their views differ, however, on the fate of the universe. There are two main theories on the subject. One holds that the expansion of the universe is not self-limited and will never cease. The galaxies will fly away from each other, space will become emptier, and eventually, stars will run out of nuclear fuel. Some will shrink, cool, and end up as black dwarfs, stars composed of cold, degenerate matter. Other stars will die as supernovae. A supernova is a stellar explosion releasing a tremendous amount of energy that creates an extremely luminous object. Debris from these explosions will crumble inward due to immense gravity and form neutron stars. Neutron stars are the collapsed cores of massive stars. Heavier neutron stars will again be crushed and shrunk due to gravity until they finally become invisible black holes. A black hole is a collapsing stellar core whose gravitational field is so powerful that nothing, including light, can escape once it has fallen past a certain point, called the event horizon. Nobody knows whether or how black holes die.

During the universe's expansion, what will be the fate of our solar system? Fusion is the combining of two light nuclei at high temperatures to form a heavier nucleus with the release of a large amount of energy. Fusion of hydrogen into helium occurs in the sun. When the hydrogen fuel gets used up, the sun will begin to contract. As a result, the nuclear fuel will become concentrated and a new series of nuclear fusion reactions will occur. The exterior of the sun will expand and cool under the combined influence of hydrogen fusion in a thin outer shell and the high temperature helium fusion in the core. The sun's atmosphere will expand into space and will be transformed into a red giant star. The sun will slowly become red and overheat the earth. As a result, the Arctic and Antarctic ice will melt, flooding the coasts of the world. The high ocean temperature will release more water vapor into the air, increasing cloudiness. The clouds will shield the earth from sunlight delaying the end a little. Eventually the oceans will boil. Billions of years from now, the distending Sun will engulf many of its planets including the earth.

Another theory rejects the above freeze death scenario for the universe and holds instead that the expansion of the universe will eventually come to a halt. When this time comes, the outward momentum of the primordial explosion and the inward pull of gravity will momentarily hold the universe in a balance. Then, gravity will pull the components of the universe together. In the currently expanding universe, the galaxies are receding from each other. This recession of the neighboring galactic systems will cease some tens of billions of years from now. The universe will start contracting. Initially the contraction will be slow, but over many billions of years, the pace will accelerate. Finally, the universe will collapse into the heat and chaos from which it emerged billions of years ago. Some astronomers believe that the universe will not reemerge from the collapsed state, while others speculate that it will rebound with a new explosion, experience a new moment of making, and become an entirely new world, in which no trace of the present universe remains.

As the collapse of the universe continues at an accelerated pace, an observer would no longer be able to spot individual galaxies because these would be fusing with each other as intergalactic space closes up. *Encyclopedia Britannica* describes the final days of our universe as follows:

[A]s the end approaches, first the galaxies, then the stars are crushed into each other in an overwhelming cataclysmic inferno in which ultimately the collapsing cosmos reverts to the primeval chaos of Big Bang.[2]

Whether the universe rises again phoenix-like from the singularity is not known. Should the universe rise again, famous astronomer Carl Sagan wonders, "What would those other universes be like? Would they be built on different laws of physics? Would they have stars and galaxies, or something quite different?"[3]

The Theory of Evolution

Life as we know it today did not exist at the birth of our universe fourteen to twenty billion years ago. And the variety of early life forms on Earth four billion years ago was not comparable to what is seen today.

How did these life forms evolve? Interactions between organic and inorganic chemicals in the early atmosphere of the earth resulted in the formation of RNA (ribonucleic acid) or DNA (deoxyribonucleic acid). The DNA was encapsulated into original prokaryotes, one-celled organisms that do not have a distinct nucleus. These grew into a metaphorical tree, whose trunk represents kingdoms, whose branches and sub-branches represent phylum, class, order, family and genus, and whose twigs represent species. Kingdom, phylum, class, order, family, genus, and species are the taxonomical classifications used in classifying plants, animals, and micro-organisms into increasingly broader categories based on shared features. Traditionally, organisms were grouped by physical resemblances, but in recent times other criteria such as genetic matching have also been used.

Biologists have constructed a scientific model to explain the origin of life, its growth in a tree-like fashion, and the underlining process for that growth. This model is the theory of evolution. The National Academy of Science defines the word "theory" as follows: a well substantiated explanation of some aspect of the natural world that can incorporate facts, laws, inferences, and tested hypotheses. When people talk about the theory of evolution, however, they are often confused about the words "theory" and "evolution." Therefore, we need to explain the scientific meaning of these words.

Stephen Jay Gould, previously of Harvard University and a leading advocate for the theory of evolution, explains the word theory as follows: "In American vernacular, 'theory' often means 'imperfect,' part of a hierarchy of confidence running downhill from fact to theory to hypothesis to guess." It is this mistaken notion of what a theory is that moves anti-evolutionists to argue that evolution is a theory and not a fact, and that it is inferior to fact. Gould clarifies further:

[Evolution] is a theory. It is also a fact, and facts and theories are different things, not rungs in a hierarchy of increasing certainty. Facts are the world's data.

Theories are structures of ideas that explain and interpret facts.

Theories connect all facts together to form an inherently consistent story. According to Gould, in science " 'fact' can only mean 'confirmed to such a degree that it would be perverse to withhold provisional assent.' " Facts that support the theory of evolution do not vanish when varying rival theories are offered to explain the process.[4]

Charles Darwin did not use the word *evolution*. The word, *evolve*, appeared, however, as the last word in his work, *The Origin of Species*. *Webster's Third International Dictionary* defines the word *evolution* as "a process of continual change from a lower, simpler, or worse condition to a higher, more complex, or better state." *The American Heritage Dictionary* defines evolution as "a gradual process in which something changes into a different or better form." Darwin himself understood the word as defined in the dictionary. The contemporary scientific definition of the word *evolution* differs greatly from Darwin's understanding and from that given in standard dictionaries. When lay people talk about the theory of evolution, however, they tend to use the meaning given by a standard dictionary. Scientists say that these definitions are simply wrong. Standard biology textbooks define evolution as any change in the frequency of alleles within a gene pool from one generation to the next. What does this mean? First, alleles are alternative variants (different versions) of the same gene. For example, humans can have A, B, or O alleles that determine one aspect of their blood type. Second, a gene pool is the set of all genes in a species or population. Finally, for geneticists, a population means a group of organisms that interbreed or have the potential to do so. The genetic composition of a certain population exists and evolves over time.

The Chemical Evolution of Life

We do not know precisely how life began on Earth. This remains a mystery. But the general scientific view is that life somehow evolved through a series of chemical reactions in oceans and ponds, which are sometimes referred to as "pre-biotic soups." However, the presence of the carbon-containing molecules, such as sugars, purines, and pyrimidines, is a precondition in order for life to emerge. Currently, these molecules are produced only by living things. How then did these pre-life chemicals come into existence?

In the 1920s, Alexander Oparin in the Soviet Union and J.B.S. Haldane in England independently introduced ideas that explained the origin of life on Earth. Later, other scientists developed a comprehensive theory that has become the cornerstone of the scientific explanation of the origin of life. They maintain that in the past, the atmosphere of the earth was much different than it is today. After the earth and the solar system were formed out of the condensation of interstellar materials, the atmosphere had an abundance of hydrogen, methane (a simpler reduced form of carbon), and ammonia (a simpler reduced form of nitrogen). New compounds were formed as a result of the exposure of the early atmosphere to lightning, radiation, volcanoes and meteors.

Rainfalls would then siphon these compounds into oceans and ponds. The chemicals in the pre-biotic soup combined and transformed into more complex compounds and ultimately into life itself. Stanley Miller and Harold Urey in the 1950s provided laboratory evidence for formation of a number of organic compounds, including several amino acids, by exposing a mixture of water, hydrogen, ammonia, and methane to electric charges for several days.

Even though there remains much dispute about the details of the origin of life in the earth's early atmosphere, there is no disagreement that nucleotides are the building blocks of deoxyribonucleic acid (DNA) and that DNA is the basis of all life on Earth. A nucleotide is composed of one five-carbon sugar (deoxyribose), one phosphoric acid radical, and one nitrogen-containing base (adenine, cytosine, guanine, or thymine). Repetition of four units of nucleotides forms a unit of DNA, the basic building block of life. Most scientists believe that the "spontaneous" formation of small molecules such as amino acids and nitrogen bases could have occurred under various earthly conditions in the past; however, they are not certain about how these molecules merged into larger units.

Even though scientists believe that life probably began in water, until recently there has been no sound explanation for the paradox of polymerization in the presence of water. Polymerization is a chemical reaction that joins small molecules into large chains of molecules. The product formed by polymerization is known as a polymer. Polymerization reactions are generally dehydrations in which molecules of water are lost in the formation of a polymer. The polymer is unstable in the presence of water. A.G. Cairns-Smith, a chemist at the University of Glasgow in Scotland, has proposed that clay minerals played an important part in the origin of life. Cairns-Smith explains that the complex composition of clay minerals facilitates the catalysis of chemical reactions. According to Cairns-Smith, absorption and concentration of molecular intermediates on clay could offset the tendency to break down the polymers of biological significance in water. Therefore, some scientists claim that clay played a role in the condensation of the sugar, phosphates, and nitrogen bases into DNA. Subsequently the DNA became more complex and organized into a living cell through a series of stages.

Another scientific claim, by Manfred Eigen, William Gardiner, Peter Schuster, and Ruthild Winkler-Oswatisch, is that the earliest genetic unit was ribonucleic acid (RNA). They assumed that RNA preceded DNA because the function of the complex DNA structure depends upon RNA. Eigen's theory posits that RNA molecules (by themselves) rearranged their structure and somehow directed themselves to a synthesis of more complex enzymes, which led to the "accidental" development of life. There is, however, no scientific consensus yet on the sequences of chemical reactions that led to the emergence of life and its first single living cell.

According to biologists, the primitive cell gradually evolved into plants and animals. This evolution was due to variations within members of a species and spontaneous beneficial mutation (a mutation is a permanent change in the DNA sequence of a gene) within the cell, and competitive struggle between members of a species to reproduce and survive in a hostile natural world. In *The Origin of Species,* Charles Darwin proposed that in nature there is a struggle for survival between organisms. He calls this struggle natural selection. Other scientists call it survival of the fittest. Darwin described the outcome of this struggle as follows: "[F]rom the war of nature, from famine and death, the most exalted object which we are capable of conceiving, namely, the production of the higher animal directly follows." He concluded that "there is grandeur in this view of life, with its general powers having been originally breathed by the Creator into few forms or into one; and that, whilst this planet has gone cycling on according to the fixed laws of gravity, from so simple a beginning endless forms, most beautiful and most wonderful have been, and are being evolved."[5]

Darwin explained the process of evolution as follows: A struggle for existence inevitably follows from the high rate at which all organic beings tend to increase [and] every organic being is striving to increase in a geometrical ratio; that each at some period of its life, during some season of the year, during each generation or at intervals, has to struggle for life and suffer great destruction. When we reflect on this struggle, we may console ourselves with full belief, that the war of nature is incessant . . . the vigorous, the healthy, and the happy survive and multiply [and] that any variation in the least degree injurious would be rigidly destroyed. This preservation of favourable individual differences and variations, and the destruction of those, which are injurious, I have called Natural Selection or the Survival of the Fittest.[6]

Since Darwin's time, biologists have discovered other factors *that could lead to speciation. G. H. Hardy and W. Weinberg, the* fathers of evolutionary mathematics, explained the mechanism of evolution as follows. A genotype is the genetic constitution of (or the totality of genes possessed by) an organism (or a group of organisms) irrespective of its physical appearance. The genotype reflects the frequency of alleles in the population. Alleles are alternative variants (different versions) of the same gene, one from each parent, for a particular Mendelian character— for example, black or white complexion—occupying the same position in a homologous chromosome. A chromatid is one of two identical copies of DNA making up a chromosome, which are joined at their constricted area called centromere. Homologous chromosomes are chromosome pairs, one from each parent, that are similar in length, gene position and centromeres location. So, evolution can be precisely defined as any change in the frequency of alleles within a gene pool from one generation to the next. A gene pool is the set of all genes in a species or population. For geneticists, a population means a group of organisms that interbreed or have the potential to do so. Hardy and Weinberg found that both allelic and genotypic frequencies remain unchanged from generation to generation unless their equilibrium is disturbed by external factors such as natural selection, mutation, migration, or genetic drift. When the equilibrium is disturbed, new species emerge.

Random selection operates in the propagation of alleles from parent population to offspring population. Human beings have no way of predicting the exact constitution of an individual offspring, but they can predict the gene pool of a certain population if mutation is excluded. When we look at the fertilization process, organisms form many more gametes (reproductive cells; egg or sperm) than those actually taking part in such fertilization. There is always a chance that an allele will be missing from those that contributed to the genetic constitution of the next generation, primarily due to sampling error (for example, random selection of one sperm out of a few million that fertilize one female egg). Thus, the gene pool changes by chance alone. The use of the term "chance" in any scientific theory is not, strictly, a rejection of causation. In fact, it is a statement about our lack of knowledge about causation. In spite of this lack of knowledge about all variables in the initial conditions, final states can be assigned certain probabilities of occurring. Such probability prediction is based on the simplest of mathematical formulas from the theory of probability.

Two predominant theories explain the patterns of evolution: the neo-Darwinian evolutionary synthesis of Ernest Mayr of Harvard University and Gould's punctuated equilibria. The modern version of the neo-Darwinian evolutionary synthetic theory holds that small mutations take place in DNA that an organism passes on to new generations, resulting in small variations—in size, strength, shape, behavior, intelligence, endurance, and so on—among the new generations. Ecological factors include natural selection screening out some combinations of mutant genes to form subspecies. Isolating mechanisms, such as geographic barriers, habitat preference, seasonal breeding, behavioral (ethological) differences, etc., prevent the subspecies (incipient species) from merging with the general populations from which they originated. Thus, natural selection, aided by the isolating mechanisms, produces viable species, i.e., species that survive in a particular environmental niche. In the words of Ernest Mayr, the evolutionary synthetic theory, or "gradual evolution... [is] explained in terms of small genetic changes (mutation) and recombination, and the ordering of this genetic variation by natural selection."[7]

The implication of classical Darwinism and neo-Darwinism is that the fossil record should reflect slowly changing forms—that the intermediate forms of life should be preserved as fossils and we should be able to unearth them. Darwin wrote in *The Origin of Species:*

I look at the geological record as a history of the world imperfectly kept, and written in a changing dialect; of this history, we possess the last volume alone, relating only to two or three countries. Of this volume, only here and there a short chapter has been preserved; and of each page, only here and there a few lines.[8]

Many more fossils have been discovered over the hundred years since Darwin's death, of course. We are no longer limited to the most recent volume, and some of the volumes are now far more complete. Nevertheless, fewer examples of gradual change have been found than might have been expected. From Darwin's time until recently, discrepancies in the model of phyletic change (phylum: a primary category in biological classification, especially of animals, that ranks above the class and below the kingdom) in the fossil record have been ascribed to imperfections in the fossil record itself. Other causes are postulated to be erosion, lack of proper conditions for fossilization, or simply not looking in the right place.

Nils Eldredge and Stephen Jay Gould have a different explanation for the morphological invariance of species through time and the unconnected intermediates in the fossil record. The theory of punctuated equilibrium by Eldredge and Gould explains the rarity, not absence, of transitional forms. Gould posits punctuated equilibria as a sound explanation for the inconsistencies of the fossil record. He dismisses the idea of gradual evolution and affirms an idea of evolution that is more comparable to "climbing a flight of stairs (punctuation and stasis) than rolling up an inclined plane." Gould states:

New species usually arise, not by the slow and steady transformation of entire ancestral populations, but by splitting off of small populations from an unaltered ancestral stock. The frequency and speed of such speciation is among the hottest topics in evolutionary theory today, but I think that most of my colleagues would advocate ranges of hundreds or thousands of years for the origin of most species by splitting.[9]

Anti-evolutionists often distort the theory of punctuated equilibrium by propagating the idea that this theory does not accept the existence of any transitional species. But the theory clearly postulates the existence of morphological intermediates as small populations. Punctuationalists claim that evolution is continuous but jerky, with established lineages. A species remains static without any morphological change. Then, a small peripheral isolated population of the species changes rapidly into a new species as a result of mutation in the regulatory gene that controls the expression of the structural gene. The new species migrates into the parent species. Gould and Eldredge have not claimed their explanation of gaps in the fossil record to be "a new discovery, but a novel interpretation for the oldest and most robust of paleontologicial observations."[10] Gould has pointed out many times that instantaneous speciation is an artifact of the compression of time that takes place each time a new layer is formed in the fossil record. The geological moments are equal to millions of years of human time frame.

Evidence for the Theory of Evolution

The fact that evolution has taken place is no longer disputed among the majority of biologists. Scientists conducting research in different branches of science have accumulated a large amount of credible evidence for the evolution of life and the theory of evolution. Some of this evidence comes from the field of paleontology, the study of life in the geological past. Paleontologists study sedimentary rocks, which are composed of sediments that gradually settled in cumulative layers at the bottom of oceans and large lakes, carrying with them the remains of plants and animals. The deepest strata of these rocks are the oldest, and the shallowest the most recent. Paleontologists have recovered and scrutinized the fossil remains of thousands of organisms that lived in the past from these sedimentary rocks, and they have arranged them according to a geological time scale. Fossil records show that many kinds of extinct organisms were different in form from those living now. They reveal successions of organisms, with simpler life forms appearing early and complex forms appearing later.

Stratigraphic dating is reliable but not absolute. It shows only the chronological order for the appearance of organisms, but does not tell the exact time of their appearance within the chronological age of the earth. Absolute dating is determined by radiometry, which uses the rate of decay of radioactive elements in the geological deposits and fossils to calculate their age. Radioactive dating has shown that the earth was formed 4.5 billion years ago. The study of fossils clearly indicates that not all forms of life originated simultaneously, nor in six earthly days, as claimed by some Muslims, Jews and Christians.

The earliest fossils of microorganisms resembling bacteria and blue algae are three to five billion years old. The oldest animal fossils are of small wormlike creatures. They are seven hundred million years old. Animals with backbones, known as vertebrates, appeared as primitive fishlike organisms four hundred million years ago and gradually evolved into modern fish. Later, amphibians and birds appeared in the fossil record. Finally, mammals appear in fossils about two hundred million years old. The most primitive, single-celled organisms are found in the oldest and deepest rocks, while chronologically younger rocks contain progressively more complex forms of life. Such a distribution and layering suggests evolution.

Comparative anatomy is the study of inherited similarities in bone structure and soft tissues among various organisms. Even without fossil evidence, we are able to infer that organisms have evolved by adapting structures of other species that still survive today. The skeletons of bats, whales, humans, and horses are remarkably similar, even though they live in different environments and have very different lifestyles. Homologous versions of different bones are found not only in the limbs of the various animals, but throughout the remainder of their bodies as well. The various homologous bones enable humans to write, bats to fly, whales to swim, and squirrels to carry and hide their food for the coming winter. The concept that each individual species emerged separately from others is not congruent with the evidence of similar bone structures found across different types of animals. Similarities of skeletal anatomies can be explained as structures inherited from common ancestors and modified to adapt to the different environments and ways of life that each species had to deal with.

Further evidence of common ancestral species comes from studying the development of animal embryos. The early embryos of vertebrates such as fish, birds, lizards, and mammals (including humans) are strikingly similar. That most animals develop gill slits below their heads suggests that these animal embryos may have descended from ancestral species that lived in the water. Similarly, across different species, structures analogous to the bones of the forehand develop from the same region of the embryo. Moreover, vertebrate embryos initially have tails. In certain species (including humans), tails disappear as embryos mature, except in some extremely rare cases in which human babies are born with tails. This common developmental pattern across various species of animals and humans reflects our evolutionary kinship within the animal kingdom.

I am a physician by profession. My medical education and experience from my professional life provide me convincing evidence to accept the human species as a product of evolution. Vestigial organs are structures that are greatly reduced, often without any function in the body. Such vestiges of the embryonic rudiments are common in all sorts of animals, including human beings. For example, in mammals that have a coarse diet with considerable amounts of cellulose, a part of the large intestine called the caecum forms a large sac in which mixtures of food and enzymes can react for a long period of time; a constricted appendix is absent altogether. But in human beings the caecum is modified into an appendix. The nictitating membrane of the eyes is another example. All tetrapods (four-footed animals) have a nictitating membrane in the inner corner of the eye. In most vertebrates, this membrane sweeps clear across the eyeball to cleanse it. In birds this membrane is particularly well developed. In horses and other mammals, it is well developed and fully functional. But in humans and some other mammals, it forms a mere fold at the inner corner of the eye and has no function. The human external ear muscles present a similar situation. Many mammals move the external ear freely in order to detect sounds efficiently. The complete muscular apparatus for these movements is present in man, but it has no function. The human coccyx at the end of the sacrum is a vestige of a tail that reflects our common genetic heritage with other mammals. Many cases of babies born with tails have been reported in the medical literature.

Likewise, vestigial characters should also be found at the molecular level. Humans do not have the capability to synthesize Vitamin C. However, the presumed ancestors of humans and most other animals except primates and guinea pigs had this function. The presence of this lost function to synthesize Vitamin C as a molecular vestigial character in humans, other primates, and guinea pigs would be an irrefutable defense for the theory of evolution. Not surprisingly for most biologists, the gene required for Vitamin C synthesis was found in guinea pigs, humans, and other primates as a non-functioning gene, thereby providing an even stronger case for the theory of evolution.

Another familiar example of natural selection occurs at the bacterial level. Pediatricians encounter unhappy parents almost daily when they do not prescribe anticipated antibiotics for their children with viral infections. Doctors do not prescribe unnecessary antibiotics because antibiotics do no good to people sick with viral infection. In fact, prescribing antibiotics for viral infections would actually cause harm, because the unnecessary antibiotics help antibiotic-resistant bacteria to survive and multiply selectively. It should be emphasized that the antibiotic does not *cause* the bacteria to develop resistance. Rather, in the environment containing antibiotics, the antibiotic-resistant strain survives while its antibiotic-sensitive "siblings" perish altogether. Consequently, the antibiotic-resistant strain survives to pass on this trait to subsequent generations.

Another example is that of sickle cell anemia. Sickle cell anemia is a hereditary disease of many African and Mediterranean people. Hemoglobin is a molecule that carries oxygen in the red blood cells. Most people have hemoglobin A in the red blood cells while people with sickle cell anemia carry hemoglobin S. The sickle cell gene that causes sickle cell anemia is very common (15–30 percent of the population) in areas of Africa where malignant falciparum malaria is endemic. This is because people with the sickle cell trait are more resistant to malaria than people with normal hemoglobin A. Not only do those with the sickle cell trait survive malaria at a greater rate than those who have normal hemoglobin A, they pass this trait on to their offspring. Furthermore, the institution of slavery brought Africans with sickle cell trait to America. It is reasonable to assume that the early American black population had a high incidence of the sickle cell trait, comparable to those who lived in their ancestral natural habitat in Africa. Malaria was eradicated from America very recently. According to the theory of evolution, the frequency of hemoglobin S in the American black population should decline in the absence of strong selective force (malaria), and that is exactly what is happening today. The incidence of sickle trait among black Americans has declined to 8 percent.

The universal presence of DNA in every form of life on the earth except in viruses (viruses may contain either DNA or RNA as their genetic material), is an important piece of evidence for evolution. It is made out of phosphate, sugar, and four bases: adenine (A), cytosine (C), guanine (G), and thymine (T). These bases can be thought of as a four-letter alphabet or code. Just as words in our language differ according to the sequence of letters of the alphabet, a specific sequence of nucleotides encoded in a DNA strand determines the uniqueness of a gene; and combinations and permutations of genes in the chromosome decide the nature and shape of life forms on Earth. The study of chromosomes quite convincingly points out that all organisms, from bacterium to human, have chromosomes that are made out of the same substance. Molecularly they differ only in relation to the specific sequence of nucleotides encoded in a DNA strand and the combinations of genes in each chromosome, as well as the number of chromosomes in each cell. This unity in diversity suggests the genetic continuity and common ancestry of all organisms.

Similarly, the shared biochemistry and physiology between and among all forms of life uphold the shared evolutionary origin. When we compare the biochemistry of different species, we encounter similar biochemical pathways working across all life forms. All known organisms use extremely similar, if not identical, metabolic pathways and metabolic enzymes in processing energy-containing molecules. For example, the metabolic systems in living organisms use glycolysis, which is the breakdown of a compound such as glycogen or glucose by enzymes, producing pyruvic or lactic acid and releasing energy for use in the body, the citric acid cycle, and oxidative phosphorylation, in which a phosphate group is added to an organic molecule to produce an organic phosphate. In all eukaryotes (i.e., any organism with one or more cells that have visible nuclei and organelles) and in the majority of prokaryotes (i.e., organisms whose DNA is not contained within a nucleus), glycolysis is performed in the same ten steps, in the same order, using the same ten enzymes. In addition, the most basic unit of energy storage, the adenosine triphosphate molecule (ATP), is the same in all species that have been studied. Such metabolic similarity between species adds more evidence for the theory of evolution. The theory of evolution would have been discredited if modern biochemical discoveries did not concur with the anatomical, biochemical, palaeontological, and other evidences for evolution. The evidence of evolution presented above is but a small portion of examples too numerous to include here.

Universally, biologists do not agree on all features of evolution. The overwhelming majority, however, agree that the different forms of life did not all originate simultaneously. They also agree that in the early biography of life, organisms were much less complex and that over a period of 3.5 billion years on the earth, increasingly complex life forms emerged. Similarly, almost all biologists concur that organisms can be traced to a single DNA collection or family, based upon the overwhelming evidence of later organisms having evolved from their earlier ancestors. At the same time, evolutionists readily admit that details of such origination and the mechanisms of the transformation of simple organisms into multitudes of species is still a matter of debate. Such is the nature of the scientific enterprise.

NOTES

1. http://www.time.com/time/magazine/article/0,9171,953088-2,00.html.

2. Hardy, Edward R. 1981. "Origin and Evolution of the Universe." *Encyclopaedia Britannica*, Macropaedia. 15th ed. Vol. 18, 1011.

3. Sagan, Carl. 1980. *Cosmos*. New York: Random House. 267.

4. Ashley, Montagu, editor, *Science and Creationism*, "Evolution as Fact and Theory," Stephen Jay Gould. 1984. Oxford, New York, Toronto: Oxford University Press. 118–119.

5. Darwin, Charles. *The Origin of Species*. 1958. New York, Scarborough: New American Library. 450.

6. Ibid. pp 75, 86, 88.

7. Mayr, Ernst, William Provine, editors. 1981. *The Evolutionary Synthesis*. "Prologue:
Some Thought on the History of the Evolutionary Synthesis." Cambridge, Massachusetts, and London, England: Harvard University Press. 1.

8. Darwin, Charles. *The Origin of Species*. 312.

9. Gould, Stephen Jay. "A quahog is a quahog." *Natural History*,

August-September 1979, 18–26.

10. Gould, Stephen Jay, and Nile Eldredge. "Punctuated Equilibrium Comes of Age." *Nature* 336, 1993. 223–227.

Part Three

How have you reconciled science's theory of evolution with the scriptures of your faith?

In his answer to our first question, Dr. Van Till provided a useful framework for the analysis of scientific questions and then focused his analysis on the big picture: cosmic evolution. Rabbi Kay focused on a subset of cosmic evolution: biological evolution. Dr. Shanavas added to these perspectives by discussing aspects of both cosmic and biological evolution. Regardless of their individual focus, the perspectives of these Christian, Jewish and Muslim scientists about the theory of evolution were consistent with each other.

Now, Dr. Van Till, Rabbi Kay and Dr. Shanavas will answer our second question and explain why they believe in the compatibility of that theory and the scriptures of their faiths.

A Case for Realistic Respect
By Howard J. Van Till

By treating the Christian Scriptures with the kind of respect that I believe they deserve, I find these revered writings of the Judeo-Christian tradition to be inspiring in my quest to enrich the human experience and encouraging in my search for the meaning and significance of what science has learned about life's evolution on Earth. In order to practice this respect, however, I find that I must resist the temptations either to idolize the text or to make unrealistic demands on it. Specifically, I find that I must refrain from expecting or forcing the biblical text to provide answers to modern scientific questions that are wholly foreign to the very nature of the Scriptures.

The Scriptures of the Christian Faith

A particular religious community can usually be identified by the literature that it has chosen to serve as its Scriptures — the collection of writings considered by that community to be both authoritative (providing incontestable and trustworthy standards for true belief and correct practice) and sacred (holy, entitled to be revered as special writings because of their connection with the God who is worshipped by that community of faith). For the Christian community into which I was born, the Scriptures consist of the familiar combination of the Old Testament, derived from the Jewish Scriptures, and the New Testament with its focus on Jesus and the early Christian community.

The Old Testament of the Christian Bible is closely related to the Jewish Scriptures, especially to the early Greek translation known as the Septuagint, but the various books that comprise it are ordered and grouped differently. The twenty-four books of the Jewish Bible (grouped into three sections — the Law, the Prophets and the Writings) have been rearranged and divided into thirty nine books. The Christian New Testament is made up of the Gospels, variations on a collection of stories about Jesus; the Acts of the Apostles, a selective history of the early Christian church; the Epistles, letters written to early Christian groups or individuals; and the book of Revelation, highly dramatic apocalyptic literature. In the Roman Catholic and Eastern Orthodox communities these books are supplemented with a collection commonly called the *Apocrypha*, writings held to be important to the Jewish community and incorporated into the Greek Septuagint that was so influential in the early Christian Church and in the formation of the Christian canon.

The Range of Christian Concepts of the Nature of Scripture

Respectful Disagreement

I think that it is safe to presume that all members of the Christian community hold their Bible in high esteem. But most Christians, I believe, would wish to clarify and strengthen that statement by adding that the Bible is held in high esteem for one very particular reason: it is an extraordinary book that deserves respect because it was in some substantial way inspired by God and therefore has the nature of divine revelation. As the "Word of God," the Bible is taken to be wholly trustworthy in what it teaches and to speak with divine authority on matters of faith and conduct. One particular segment of the Christian community, however, would make an even stronger claim: the Bible is authoritative and infallible not only on matters of theology and human behavior, but on all subjects to which it makes any reference at all. To this portion of the Christian community, often designated as Conservative Evangelical or Fundamentalist, the Bible is considered to be comprehensively "inerrant"—without error of any kind—on matters of theology, human behavior, church administration, history and many other subjects, even on questions that can now be framed only in the conceptual vocabulary of modern science.

Clearly, then, the way in which a Christian applies the Scriptures to questions raised by modern science (questions regarding the evolutionary history of the universe, for instance) will vary greatly according to one's concept of the nature and authority of these Scriptures. On this issue there are huge disagreements within the Christian community and it would be wholly misleading to speak as if Christians were in full accord concerning the nature of the Bible and its relevance to scientific theorizing. For that reason readers of this book must understand that I make no pretense of speaking for the entire Christian community regarding the way in which scientific theories of evolution might be reconciled to the Bible. The best that I can do is to speak candidly about how my personal approach has developed over the years and, from time to time, to indicate how it compares to other Christian approaches.

Three Options for Christians

For the sake of this discussion, let me identify and name what I see as the three principal ways in which various portions of the larger Christian community view the nature and appropriate use of the Christian Scriptures:

1. The Bible as religiously insightful literature: Christians holding this view would posit that it is appropriate and important to respect the

Scriptures as insightful religious writings, inherited from the historic Christian community, that provide us with a basic knowledge of our religious heritage and an informed sense of our religious identity. But they would also be inclined to argue that there is no substantive warrant for making additional assertions regarding divine authorship, divine authority, instructional infallibility or comprehensive inerrancy of the Bible.

2. The Bible as an inspired and infallible guide: Christians holding this view would affirm that it is both necessary and warranted to view the Scriptures as divinely inspired, authoritative, trustworthy and infallible guides for matters of faith and conduct. At the same time, however, holders of this view would consider it a mistake to overlook the time-bound nature of the biblical writers' knowledge of history, science, and the like. Specific theories of divine inspiration and particular implications of the Bible's historical, cultural and religious contexts vary considerably among the members of this broad category.

3. The Bible as a comprehensively inerrant authority: Christians holding this view would insist that it is both necessary and warranted to view the Bible, in its entirety, not only as a divinely inspired, authoritative and infallible guide for matters of faith and practice, but also as being inerrant in whatever it says on any topic, including topics to which the modern natural sciences are now especially relevant. Declarations regarding the comprehensive inerrancy and divine authority of the Bible are generally given high visibility in statements of faith for Christian groups who hold this belief concerning the nature of their Holy Scriptures.

The Evolution of my Concept of Scripture: An Ongoing Journey

Born into a Heritage

Most members of the Calvinist community into which I was born were content with a working concept of Scripture in the general vicinity of the second of the three options stated above. The Bible was considered to be divinely inspired in the sense that the human writers of the text were guided by the Holy Spirit (in a manner beyond human comprehension) to write in such a way that the biblical text—when responsibly interpreted—was, and remains, infallible and authoritative on matters of religious faith and human conduct. Obvious differences in writing style and knowledge base were attributed to the individual writers and to their historical context without apparent threat to the effectiveness of divine inspiration. Specifically, the non-scientific character of the creation narratives was recognized by the majority of my denomination, although a vocal minority often criticized that judgment and leaned strongly in the direction of the comprehensive inerrancy option listed above.

For most of my lifetime, I was reasonably content with the majority perspective of my community. I found comfort and reassurance in having Scriptures that were in some way set above ordinary writings but still open to responsible interpretive efforts and not bound to the additional requirement of being inerrant on matters of modern science. This concept of the Scriptures seemed appropriate and workable to me, and it was strongly reinforced by the majority of the people with whom I regularly interacted as a member of the faculty of the college operated by my denomination.

Defending the Received View

My acceptance of this perspective, even a rather right-leaning version of it, was firmly in place early in my life. In my senior year at a private Christian high school I wrote an essay entitled, "The True Defense of Christianity." (This essay constituted my entry in a contest in which all essays had to be based on the works of conservative Calvinist theologian Cornelius van Til, the revered mentor of our Bible teacher. For this exercise in articulating the orthodox view, I was pleased to be the recipient of a First-Prize check in the sum of $25.) I opened the essay with a quotation that represented a view of Scripture that was certainly *not* welcomed in my religious community. This was the beast that had to be slain in the remainder of my essay.

> The Bible is not a book. The Bible is to be regarded as not a single volume but an anthology. Its writings represent more than a thousand years of effort by excellent story tellers, poets, artists, historians, and moral pioneers. Laboriously inscribed on skins or papyrus, the writings we have are not in their original form. As they did their recopying, scribes frequently made additions, which were later incorporated into the text, so that a single section may record the views of widely differing authors who lived in totally different eras. Indeed some Scriptural passages, far from being a unity, are almost like a debate and vividly demonstrate a legitimate diversity of opinion.[1]

My explicit rejection of this view of Scripture gave clear and unequivocal evidence that I had absorbed what I had been taught: a rather conservative perspective located somewhere between options two and three above. "This is a basic denial of the authority of the Bible and all of its teachings," I said in 1956.

It is a denial of the authority of God in His word. It is therefore a denial of our basic Christian doctrine—God's authority over man as revealed in the Bible and in nature . . . The Bible is the final authority on all the Christian truths. The Bible speaks on every aspect of God and His universe. All facts must be interpreted in relation to the Bible. Likewise all arguments in defense of Christianity must be based on the Bible.

As a consequence of consistent and effective training in the church, home and day school, that's where I was more than fifty years ago. And I stayed in the vicinity of that perspective for several decades. I attribute a substantial part of that stability to my being a member of the faculty of the Christian college owned and operated by my denomination. The received view was carefully articulated by my colleagues, and my acceptance of it was regularly reinforced as a natural consequence of my immersion in a religiously homogeneous community. For a long time I experienced neither need nor encouragement to re-examine the orthodoxy that I had inherited.

Taking the Bible Seriously in the Turmoil of Debate

By the 1980s, after many years of observing the development of the creation/evolution debate, I became increasingly annoyed at the way in which that raucous shouting match functioned to promote the idea that biblical belief and natural science were irreconcilable adversaries. In my own mind, I knew better. I was well acquainted with the scientific approach to learning about the formational history of the universe and of terrestrial life forms, and I was committed to maintaining a deep respect for the Christian Scriptures. But I experienced no deep tension between the two. In my astronomy courses, I taught freely about cosmic evolution and stellar evolution, and I also freely expressed my belief that these concepts were in no way in conflict with a Christian commitment to viewing the universe as a Creation that had been given being by the Creator.

At some point in my growing frustration with the creation/evolution debate I felt that I had to make a decision: either stop the complaining and put the battle entirely off to the side, or try to make a positive contribution to the science/religion discussion.

Bolstered by good experiences both in and out of the classroom, I chose to attempt the latter. In 1986 I published a book entitled *The Fourth Day: What the Bible and the Heavens are telling us about the Creation.*[2] The publisher's choice of the *Fourth Day* portion of the title was based on the facts that, a) day four of the Genesis 1 creation narrative spoke of the functions of the sun, moon and stars, and b) most of my scientific considerations in the book fell in the territory of astronomy.

The opening chapter of the book was titled, "Taking the Bible Seriously." I knew that in order to gain a hearing from my intended audience—Christians who held a strong view of biblical authority and who were also, in the wake of the creation/evolution debate, inclined to be anxious about the concept of evolution—it was imperative that I demonstrate a deep respect for what the Scriptures said, or didn't say, concerning the formational history of the Creation.

I opened that first chapter by stating that "this work is addressed to readers who want to take the Bible seriously," and that my purpose in saying so was "not only to establish the assumptions I am making about the knowledge and attitude of my readers but also to indicate my own attitude and goal." The remainder of the chapter was dedicated to explaining what it meant to me to "take the Bible seriously."

The first point of explanation was that we need to "affirm the true status" of the Bible as the "Word of God." But that affirmation was carefully qualified in such a way as to avoid unrealistically equating the words of the biblical text with words delivered directly from God. As I understood it, to call the Bible the "Word of God" was to affirm "that it occupies an elevated position relative to other human literature," while at the same time recognizing that "the term *Word* is being used in a metaphorical sense to acknowledge divine revelation, rather that in the restricted literal sense to indicate mere words." (*The Fourth Day*, 5) In my mind, and in the minds of most members of my denomination, divine inspiration was not to be simplistically equated with divine dictation.

The second point of explanation was dedicated to the idea that people who wish to take the Bible seriously must also recognize "the multifaceted character of Scripture." The Bible clearly displayed a great diversity in the nature of its contents, drew from a multiplicity of sources, and employed a wide variety of literary genres, including some that were certainly not intended to be taken literally in the modern sense of the term. Applying this specifically to matters of concern to scientists, I noted that:

> If we try to read a poetic or liturgical story of origins as if it were a primitive scientific report, we might see a chronicle of divine magic rather that an artistic portrait of the Creator-Creation relationship. In all cases, the failure to identify the genre of a piece of literature correctly not only prevents us from getting the real meaning but also may lead us into exacting a distorted, perhaps even grotesque, misinterpretation in its place. The loss is thereby doubled! (The Fourth Day, 11)

The third point of explanation concerned what I considered to be the principal functions of the Bible: to provide believers with "both the elements of Christian faith and the principles for Christian life" and with "testimonies and eyewitness accounts of God at work in human history and in his Creation." The fourth point focused on the need for sound interpretive principles that took full account of the distinction between the content of the biblical message and the literary vehicles (such as poetry or a liturgical story of origins) that conveyed that content (teachings) to the Bible's readers, or to those who long ago heard the text read to them in communal worship.

After *The Fourth Day*

Responses to my approach in *The Fourth Day* were, to put it mildly, highly varied. Many readers, especially those trained in theology or biblical studies, said, in effect, "Thanks for your effort to communicate this to Christians who are anxious about evolution, but your perspective on Scripture is nothing new. This has been taught in our college and seminary for a long time." I think they were entirely correct.

A small but highly vocal portion of my denomination, on the other hand, was stirred to "righteous indignation" (and sometimes to less than righteous forms of public denunciation) because some persons were convinced that I had failed to treat the whole Bible as pure divine revelation, that I had threatened the authority of Scripture by openly acknowledging the cultural conditioning of the text, and that I had allowed the term "Word of God" to have a metaphorical meaning. And, as if that were not bad enough, I had also failed to employ the Bible as a sword to slay the fire-breathing dragon of evolution. One rather idiosyncratic but very wealthy detractor took the extreme action of spending over $60,000 to buy full-page "advertisements" in the local newspaper (twenty-eight pages over a three-year period) in which he vigorously denounced what I had written in *The Fourth Day* and mercilessly berated all persons in positions of authority in the college and its supporting denomination for their failure to remove me from the college faculty.

Dealing with this and other travesties of religious expression was difficult, and in the long run it had an irreversible effect on my attitude toward traditional organized religion. A decade after the height of what I often call the *"Fourth Day* Fallout" period, I came to the realization that some of my religious beliefs, beliefs residing deep in the recesses of the unconscious mind, had moved far enough to fall outside of the theological boundaries set by the denomination. All of us on the college faculty had been required to sign a document called the *Form of Subscription* (originally adopted by the Synod of Dort in 1618–19) by which we pledged our allegiance to the Belgic Confession (1561), the Heidelberg Catechism (1563), and the Canons of Dort (1619) as documents that "fully agree with the Word of God." By 1997 I realized that I could no longer say what I had once said in my signing the *Form* thirty years earlier. Consequently, I chose to resign from the faculty and take early retirement. I remain fully convinced that it was the right thing to do.

Soon thereafter, my wife and I moved to a new location, left the denomination and joined an "independent, liberal church" that welcomed the kind of theological exploration that I found to be essential and invigorating.

Respecting Scripture in a New Way

One of the things that had changed within me was my concept of Scripture. As I have already indicated, I was for a long time comfortable with viewing the Bible as an inspired and infallible guide for faith and practice. In recent years, however, my view of the Scriptures has moved in the direction of option 1) in the list above—viewing the Bible as insightful religious writings inherited from the historic Christian community. When asked to specify my concept of the Bible now, as often happens in the Q&A session after a public presentation on science and religion, I usually respond with a statement something like this: I view the Bible as a thoroughly human testimony to the authentic human experience of living in the presence of the Sacred; more specifically, the Bible is the human testimony to the Sacred as experienced by the ancient Hebrew and early Christian communities.

Why the change? Why did I move from a traditional view of Scripture as special revelation (privileged information not derivable from human knowledge or insight) delivered by supernatural inspiration (direct divine action that planted specific information into the minds of the human writers) to a view that excluded such bold claims?

Truth-Claims Need Warrant

To answer as succinctly as I can, I would say that it all boils down to the matter of warrant (evidence, reasons) for any belief, including a religious belief, and specifically including religious beliefs concerning the nature of Scripture.

In the normal course of our daily experience, we are bombarded with all manner of recommendations to believe some particular proposition—about the benefits of taking multiple vitamins, say, or about the superiority of one car maker relative to all others, or about the effectiveness of tartar-fighting toothpaste, or about why we should vote for a particular political candidate. But we know that not all propositions set before us are true, so we need to weigh the evidence and reasoning offered in support of some particular truth-claim to determine whether or not belief in that claim is warranted. Sometimes we do that unconsciously or in a rather casual manner, but if the proposition in question is highly important to us, we will (or certainly should) perform our conscious and reflective evaluation with considerable care.

Some of the truth-claims presented to us for belief are religious in nature—propositions about the nature of God, or about character of divine action, or about the nature and authority of the Scriptures. It is impossible for all of the religious propositions recommended to us to be true because some of them contradict others. So, what do we do? If religious beliefs are important to us, I would say that we owe it to ourselves to do the hard work of reflective evaluation and see what religious claims are worthy of our belief. In other words, we should test religious truth-claims in the same way that we test other truth-claims: look at the evidence to see if belief is warranted. If it is, well and good. If not, then dismiss the claim. If the evidence is unclear or inconclusive, then set the proposition aside for continuing evaluation. Blind or thoughtless acceptance of tribal orthodoxy is, in my judgment, just not acceptable. It may function to keep peace within certain kinds of religious communities, but it is no way to advance our knowledge of what is real and true.

At issue at the moment are truth-claims for propositions that assert the Bible to be radically different from ordinary human literature, to be the outcome of divine revelation, to speak with divine authority, to constitute an infallible guide to religious belief and human behavior, or even—in the extreme—to be inerrant in whatever subject matter it touches on, regardless of whether that subject is central or peripheral to the Bible's core concerns.

When Warrant Is Lacking

A decade ago I began consciously to reflect on claims of this sort and to examine the evidence commonly advanced in their support. The result: I found the evidence inadequate and unconvincing. Specifically, I find claims for the Bible to be a comprehensively inerrant authority to be wholly unwarranted. Furthermore, I have too often seen holders of this view use their particular reading of the Scriptures as a weapon with which to beat down all who disagree with their own reading of the biblical text, no matter how bizarre that reading might be. Claims of biblical inerrancy (accompanied by the implicit assertion that *my* reading is the inerrant one) generally function as discussion stoppers. Recall the familiar bumper sticker slogan: "God said it. I believe it. That settles it!"

What about the less extreme view of the Bible as an inspired and infallible guide for faith and practice? Having lived with this view for a major portion of my own career, I found this to be somewhat more attractive, but nonetheless unwarranted. Challenging questions abound. What does divine inspiration actually amount to? What is the empirical evidence that the Bible, or any particular part of it, is the product of divine inspiration, whatever that is? And, given the clear fact that we do not have the original biblical writings, how do extant and highly modified copies compare to what was first divinely inspired?

And what about the myriad of steps over centuries of time by which the particular books of today's official canon were chosen from a much larger collection of candidate writings? The Bible did not, of course, drop from the skies complete and in final form.

Neither was the biblical canon written at one time by a single writer or by a coordinated team of writers. No, it is well known that the Bible is a collection of texts written over more than a thousand years of time by numerous and diverse writers having highly varied agendas. (Ironically, the author that I quoted disapprovingly in my 1956 essay was absolutely correct.) Furthermore, these texts were subject to many cycles of selection and editorial modification by other community leaders, each with a set of agendas related to the particular religious and political concerns of the day. Was that historical selection process also divinely directed? Was editing and copying also divinely inspired? And what is the evidence for that?

To make a long story short: I just don't see anything closely resembling sufficient warrant for the traditional claims regarding the Bible as a divinely inspired and infallible guide on matters of Christian faith and practice. Many people will find this disappointing.

Some will label it "heretical." Some will judge that I have "lost the faith." But my personal experience in arriving at this position has been quite the opposite. To me it feels like a load has been taken off my shoulders. No longer must I bear the implied responsibility for cleverly rationalizing claims that I must have sensed, deep inside my unconscious mental machinery, could not be warranted.

Both Treasured and Flawed

Without a doubt there are many beautiful passages in the Scriptures, passages that inspire readers to lofty thoughts, exemplary behavior and enriched lives. And the Scriptures are filled with magnificent portraits of a magnanimous and merciful God. But the same Holy Book also contains passages that turn the stomach with vivid, humanly crafted accounts that portray God as a ruthless tyrant and a zealous deity who commanded the slaughter of innocent people whose only fault was being born into the wrong tribe. No longer must I pretend that these passages are not what they appear to be; no longer must I rationalize them with pious excuses for divine terrorism. Some of the portraits of God found on the pages of the Bible are toxic and must not be taken as normative or binding.

Nonetheless, I do wish to give the Bible the respect that it deserves. These Scriptures have had an immense influence on human culture around the globe. They have preserved the wisdom of profoundly insightful people in the ancient Hebrew and early Christian communities. They have inspired all manner of commendable acts of human kindness, generosity and compassion in the name of the God of whom these Scriptures most often speak. Unfortunately, the opposite has also been the case. That reality must be humbly acknowledged and allowed to temper all human tendencies to idolize the Scriptures as incontestably perfect and to pretend that the Bible's historical application has been without blemish. We are imperfect people who have written an imperfect book.

The freedom to be realistic, and the freedom to say so, sometimes overwhelms me. The freedom to respect the Bible as an authentically human document, warts and all, is one freedom I will never relinquish. These freedoms, deeply rooted in realistic respect for the Scriptures, are freedoms that enrich the experience of life and nourish a sense of integrity.

Three Scriptural Perspectives on the Evolving Universe Concept

Early in this chapter we acknowledged the diversity of Christian perspectives on the nature of the Scriptures and described three views to represent the range of those Christian perspectives:
1. the Bible as religiously insightful literature
2. the Bible as an inspired and infallible guide and
3. the Bible as a comprehensively inerrant authority

From each of these three there will follow differing attitudes toward the scientific concept of evolution, especially toward biological evolution because it places the human species in close relationship to all other forms of life. As a means of illustrating how one's concept of the Scriptures might influence one's attitude toward evolution, suppose we were to direct the following question to each of the three representative views: Can a universe that is capable of evolving still be a Creation? This may sound like a rather peculiar question, but let's try to make some sense out of it.

If the Bible is Comprehensively Inerrant

Let us begin by directing our question to persons who hold the Bible to be a comprehensively inerrant authority on all matters of which it speaks, including matters of direct interest to modern science. On the basis of decades of experience with representatives of this view, here's how I would expect the brief conversation to go: Can a universe that is capable of evolving still be a Creation? No, of course not! If the universe were capable of evolving, then the system of natural causes would be sufficient to bring about the formation of every species of life and there would be no need for a Creator to act supernaturally. Once the unformed matter of the universe had been brought into being from nothing at the beginning, the essence of divine creative action was to endow that matter with the specific forms that God intended it to have. If species could evolve into those forms naturally, there would be no need for God to perform supernatural, form-conferring acts of special creation (forming each biological species independently) of the sort clearly and authoritatively revealed in Genesis 1. Remember, God said it. I believe it. That settles it!

Sometimes this view is supported by claims that there is empirical evidence that the system of natural causes is demonstrably inadequate, so that the complete evolutionary scenario developed by the sciences is just plain impossible. In decades past, it was "Creation-Science" that claimed both biblical and empirical support for a recent creation (six–ten thousand years ago) of a mature universe; now it is the "Intelligent Design" movement arguing (from empirical considerations alone, without explicit biblical reference) for an old-universe version of special creation.

If the Bible Is an Inspired and Infallible Guide

Since there is little encouragement for further discussion with those who preach biblical inerrancy, let's move on and direct our peculiar question to a different group of persons — those who view the Bible as an inspired and infallible guide for faith and practice. In this case we will find a theological tradition that places considerable value on maintaining a clear distinction between the Creation (the created world) and the Creator who gave it being. In fact, in talking about the divine action of creating, there would be considerably less emphasis on the idea of form-imposing intervention and more on the uniquely divine action of giving being to the whole integrated system of the universe. Rather than insisting on saying that the universe was created (thereby directing attention to particular actions in the distant past), there will be more of an inclination to say that the universe is God's Creation (thereby directing attention to the Creator-Creation relationship that is equally important at all times).

To say that the universe is a Creation, then, is to say that it is something that has being (exists) only because the Creator-God has given it being and continues to sustain it in being. Some would argue that this also implies the doctrine of *creatio ex nihilo*—creation from nothing. Some would add that this classical Christian doctrine is at least supported by the Scriptures, even if it is not explicitly taught.

Let's set some of those differences aside and focus on the core affirmation, based on biblical guidance, that the universe is a Creation and see where it leads us. Here's a sequence of inferences that, in my judgment, directly follow:

- If the universe is a Creation, then every aspect of its being—everything that it is, and everything that it is capable of doing—is a gift from the Creator.
- Every natural capability resident in the basic components of the universe must then be appreciated and celebrated as a gift of being from the Creator.
- This applies to every one of the universe's formational capabilities—each and every natural capability for forming new structures (atoms, molecules, stars, planets, bacteria, finches, humans, etc.) from the raw materials and functioning structures present at the time.
- If the Creation is capable of evolving new forms in the manner now envisioned by the natural sciences, it must have been endowed from the beginning with an astoundingly rich set of resources, formational capabilities and potentialities for functional structures.
- A Creation capable of evolving new forms in the manner of the universe of which we are a part gives evidence for the Creator's astounding creativity in envisioning a system of resources, capabilities and potentialities that would make evolution possible, and unfathomable generosity in giving such richness of being to the Creation.

Can a universe that is capable of evolving still be a Creation? Of course it can! In fact, one could well ask: How could anything but a Creation have the astounding richness of being that is necessary to enable it to evolve? How could anything but a Creation be a Right Stuff Universe?

This view is what I have called, for reasons that should be apparent, the Fully Gifted Creation Perspective. It is the view that I long promoted in my teaching career and it is the one that I continue to recommend as the best approach for persons who are wholly committed to traditional

Christian theology and who remain most comfortable with viewing the Bible as an infallible guide for faith and practice.

If the Bible Is Religiously Insightful Literature

Holders of this view of Scripture will undoubtedly approach the reconciliation of evolution with Scripture in a wide diversity of ways. Without a need to protect historic creeds or traditional dogmas, thoughtful persons will be able to offer many different approaches to the integration of the Bible's religious insights and science's theorizing about the universe's evolutionary history.

In order to illustrate my own present approach, I think it most appropriate to offer a sample of recent work in this area. In the present circumstance the choice of sample is easy. My wife and I are active members of a church formerly named Christ Community Church (CCC), located in Spring Lake, Michigan. CCC changed its name to C3 Exchange as part of a broad effort to be more inclusive and respectful of religious diversity--a goal in full harmony with the approach taken in this book. In February and March of 2008, as an illustration of what CCC understands to be appropriate activity for Progressive Christianity, we offered an online course on "Genesis and Evolution." Over a three-week period, subscribers received by e-mail a new study-unit each weekday morning. Online feedback and conversation among all participants and instructors was encouraged. Two of the study-unit writers were trained pastors (CCC pastor Ian Lawton and his father, Bill Lawton, retired priest from the Anglican Church of Australia) and their contributions focused on religious, historical, literary and pastoral concerns. My contributions focused more on questions concerning the relevance of scientific theorizing in the arenas of cosmic and biological evolution.

In one of the first lessons, Bill Lawton developed the idea that the early chapters of the book of Genesis can be fruitfully described as "storied theology"—creative narratives built on the foundation of recited stories that are historical in the sense of authentically representing the way the world was understood by the Hebrews of that time in history, but even more importantly, stories that are theological in the sense of illustrating that the ancient Hebrew understanding of the world at that time centered on the experienced immanence of the Sacred and celebrated the intimacy of relationship conceived to hold among God, world and humanity.

Because of the importance of the term "storied theology," let me quote a few excerpts from Bill Lawton's reflections on its character and function:

The text of Genesis is first spoken word. The tribes who sat around ancient campfires retold their stories of dream-time and shaped answers to an unknown and often threatening world. The stories helped make sense of chaos and carved certainties into the fabric of their lives.

Genesis is *storied theology* that captures the human longing to understand the "self."

Wonder and imagination are the human tools that create order and enable an end to chaos; wonder and imagination shape people and gods in intelligible form. But always something more teases the senses. Words are never quite adequate to assess the connections. So poetry, mythology, art, religion, loving and holding and sharing — each Adam looking into the eyes of another Eve — awaken the senses to something yet to be discovered. This is the magic of life that the storied theology of Genesis seeks to decode.

Against that background, following are my four study-units, very lightly edited wherever I judged that a bit of clarification might be helpful. Each lesson opens with brief quotations and closes with a few questions intended to stimulate further reflection. I offer these as illustrations of, a) how a person who respects the Christian Scriptures need have no difficulty in valuing what the natural sciences have learned about the formational history of the universe and the evolution of life on Earth, and b) how a person who finds theories of evolution scientifically convincing could profitably look to the Scriptural heritage for ways to discern the meaning of this remarkable drama of our formational history.

A Contemporary View: Four Lessons on Genesis and Evolution

Lesson One: Whence the Cosmos?

In the beginning Elohim created the heavens and the earth. Genesis 1:1

The Bible reflects different notions current in Israel, some of which awaken memories of ancient Near Eastern mythologies . . . It should be obvious that by the nature of things, none of these (early Genesis) stories can possibly be the product of human memory, nor in any modern sense of the word scientific accounts of the origin and nature of the physical world.

—Nahum Sarna, *Understanding Genesis*, 1, 2[3]

The Bible: An Authentically Human Document

I admire candor, so let's begin this reflection on a candid note. As I see it, the text of Genesis 1–11, like the rest the biblical text, is a thoroughly human construction and not a divinely authored revelation that delivered privileged information to one specially favored tribe. This is not what I was taught as a young lad, but it's a point of view that I now hold comfortably as a seasoned adult.

More specifically, I believe that Genesis 1–11 represents the thoughtful reflection of the ancient Hebrews concerning, a) humanity, b) the world of which humanity is a member, and c) whatever Ultimate Reality makes possible the wonder of the human experience. As such, these ancient reflections bear all of the marks of their historical, cultural and religious contexts.

The Bible: A Wealth of Storied Theology

Living in their time and place, the Hebrews developed and employed a rich tradition of "storied theology," creatively crafted stories shaped by a deeply theological agenda, that functioned to convey their solemn conjectures about the natures of God, humanity and the world and about how these three related to one another.

Most of Israel's neighbors were polytheistic. The people of the ancient Near East posited the existence and action of numerous gods who played the roles of providers/protectors of nations, of tribes, of cities, or of families. Some of their more powerful gods were experienced as the awesome and sometimes threatening powers of the environment: storms, seas, rivers, and living things endowed with the amazing power of fertility. Especially powerful were the gods of the sky: sun, moon, planets and stars.

The myths of that era were often focused on how the various gods came into being (many gods were taken to be the offspring of other gods), or how they related to one another (a common story line was "the gods of my tribe are stronger and better than the gods of *your* tribe").

Genesis 1 Then: No Gods but God

Genesis 1 opens with the simple declaration, "In the beginning Elohim created the heavens and the earth." Why the choice of "Elohim," which can also refer to the pantheon of all Ancient Near Eastern gods, rather than one of the names such as YHWH or Adonai, more unique to the covenant God of Israel? Commentators differ in their explanations, but for me this choice suggests that what follows is a bit of storied theology whose function was similar to the function of other god-stories of the day — the mythical tales of Israel's polytheistic neighbors.

Nonetheless, the specific content of the Genesis 1 narrative is unusual for its day. First, there is no mythical account of the origin or birth of Elohim. This God's existence is simply taken for granted; no further explanation required. Second, the entire array of environmental powers—every single occupant of "the heavens and the earth"—is stripped of the divine nature often assigned to them by ancient mythology. Even the lofty sun, moon and stars lost their elevated status as sky-gods. As nothing more than members of the Creation, these celestial luminaries are not to be worshiped in the way Israel's neighbors did.

Genesis 1 Now: Ancient Wisdom, Not Divine Science

What shall we do with the Genesis 1 story today? Ignore it as a piece of obsolete, irrelevant text? Oh, heavens (and earth), no. This is the text of the Judeo-Christian tradition in which we stand. This is the story that we remember as well as any story from our heritage.

But what shall we do with it? Shall we idolize it as if it were none other than a supernatural revelation? And what about that seven-day structure? Isn't that a clue that the story constitutes an answer to questions about what happened and when? Oh, yes, we know that the "days" must have represented something other than the usual twenty-four-hour thing, but that reference to the "beginning" has got to be what scientists call the big bang, right?

In my candid judgment, wrong, wrong, wrong. This wonderful bit of dramatized theology should never be mistaken for some primitive version of Big Bang cosmology. Respect for the text would, I believe, preclude such a mistake. If you want to learn something about what happened and when, good; then go to the literature of scientific cosmology and see what science has found out about the formational history of the universe. You will find a fascinating story about 13.7 billion years of evolution from a hot Big Bang beginning to an unimaginably rich array of structures from atoms to molecules, galaxies, stars, planets and living things.

If, on the other hand, you want to get a sense of how ancient Hebrew religious wisdom dealt with questions like, Why is there something instead of nothing? or, Why is the something that does exist so remarkable as to make the human experience possible? then go to Genesis 1. The answers of ancient wisdom are open to review, of course, but the determined courage of ancient sages to grapple with the Big Questions remains admirable and deserves our deepest respect.

Questions for Further Reflection

1. Can you trace the development of your own concept of God? Of creation? Of Bible?
2. Why do you think the first creation story in Genesis has a seven-day structure? To answer what-happened-when questions? To provide poetic structure? To reinforce Sabbath observance?

3. Do you think the Universe is all there is? If so, are God and Universe the same?
4. Panentheism posits: The Universe is within God, but God is more than Universe. Do you find this helpful in relating God and Universe?

Lesson Two: Let There Be Sky-Lights and Critters.

And God said, Let there be lights in the expanse of the sky to separate the day from the night . . . God made two great lights, the greater light to govern the day and the lesser light to govern the night. He also made the stars.

And God said, Let the waters teem with living creatures, and let birds fly above the earth across the expanse of the sky.

And God said, Let the land produce living creatures according to their kinds: livestock, creatures that move along the ground, and wild animals, each according to its kind.

—Excerpts from Genesis 1:14–24

Concordism: the Guarantor of Biblical Truth?

In my lifetime I've read bookshelves of writings that reduce this celebrative series of "And God said" vignettes into science like chronicles of what happened and when in the formational history of sky-things and earth-things. The technical term for this style of interpreting early Genesis is concordism. Its goal is to demonstrate a concord (agreement) between the biblical narratives and what actually took place in the sky and on the earth.

Why would major portions of the Christian community expect, or work so hard to contrive, this kind of agreement? Proponents of concordism are usually very honest and candid about their motivation. Stated bluntly, the driving force of concordism is this: "If the very first chapter of the Bible isn't true (where *true* is here reduced to mean scientifically accurate), then why should anyone believe the rest of the Bible?"

Concordism: A Failed Strategy

But concordism doesn't work, of course. The achievement of apparent concord would require that two serious violations be overlooked: First, concordism must violate the biblical text by approaching these narratives as if they were written, not as storied theology in typical ancient Near Eastern style, but as matter-of-fact chronicles that would satisfy our modern scientific curiosity about the world's formational history.

Only within the last couple of centuries could such a curiosity be seriously pursued. I have no doubt that the ancient Hebrews were fully aware that chronological accounts of sky-history or earth-history were far beyond their cognitive grasp. We would be doing neither the Hebrews nor the Scriptures any favor by reading a modern scientific agenda into an authentic sample of ancient Near Eastern religious wisdom.

Second, concordism must violate the conclusions of modern science. If Genesis 1, for example, were treated as a chronicle of the Creation's formational history, then concordism would require that the historical sciences come up with a chronological account consistent with it. The sequence of appearances that would have to be forced on the sciences is this: first, day and night; second, sky and water; third, land and seas; fourth, sun, moon and stars; fifth, fish and birds; sixth, livestock, slithering things, wild animals and humankind.

Sorry, but a competent analysis of actual data could not possibly be twisted to agree with that sequence of appearances. An honest reading of observations and measurements by persons trained to read them yields something very different.

Science and Theology, Beginnings and Evolutions

The formational history of our universe can be traced back 13.7 billion years to a super-hot big bang beginning. Was that an absolute beginning, from nothing? Was the big bang what theologians call *creatio ex nihilo*? Science has no final answer. If anything existed before the big bang it is simply not accessible to our observation. However, for reasons drawn from both theology and science, I would be very surprised if the big bang were an *ex nihilo* beginning.

What makes more sense to me theologically is the idea that there has always been God-plus-a-World, with the understanding that the God-World relationship is so intimate that neither one could be what it is without its interaction with the other. In that context the big bang would be the beginning of our particular universe, but not the beginning of all worlds related to God.

Meanwhile back in our world, lots of interesting structures took shape in the course of time. During the first two billion years after time-zero the hundreds of billions of galaxies that comprise our visible universe (what we are able to see) formed from the cooled-off remnants of the primeval fireball. Within these galaxies hundreds of billions of nuclear-powered stars formed, most of them orbited by cooler blobs of matter (like planets) that were by-products of the star formation drama.

Our sun is an ordinary, "garden variety" star in one spiral arm of the Milky Way Galaxy. Earth is one of several planets orbiting the sun. The solar system (the sun plus planets and various other lumps of matter in orbit around it) formed about 4.6 billion years ago. On Earth's surface, oceans and continents have formed, reformed and slowly drifted into their present arrangement.

Meanwhile, a drama even more fascinating began about 3.8 billion years ago: life forms appeared and evolved on Earth. Even primitive forms of life were a marvel. And the modern, complex and specialized organisms that comprise our ecosystems today are truly mind boggling.

Storied Theology for Today?

Back to the storied theology of Genesis One: "And God saw all that He had made, and it was very good." The Hebrews portrayed God eloquently in the artistically rich vocabulary of their day. We could, I suppose, content ourselves with saying as they said—repeating their words, written in their ancient context.

But I think I have an even better idea. Instead of simply saying as they said, what if we challenged ourselves to be doing as they did—using the vocabulary and knowledge of our time and place to craft a storied theology that expressed *our* awe of the human experience and *our* amazement that it is even possible? God, wouldn't that be good too?

Questions for Further Reflection

1. Is it important to you that the Genesis narratives and today's scientific theories match up?
2. In your judgment, how should scientific theories and religious text interact?
3. How significant is the idea of creation from nothing to you?
4. How would you write a storied theology relevant to the origin and formation of our universe?

Lesson Three: Formed from the Dust.

And God said, "Let the land produce living creatures according to their kinds."
—Genesis 1: 24a
When the Lord God made the earth and the heavens . . . and no shrub of the field had yet appeared on the earth and no plant of the field had yet sprung up . . . the Lord God formed the man from the dust of the ground and breathed into his nostrils the breath of life, and the man became a living being.
—Excerpted from Genesis 2:4–7

Special Creation: A Concept Rooted in Plato

During the century preceding Darwin's blockbuster book, *The Origin of Species* (1859), it was not unusual to find the concept of special creation incorporated into scientific theories about the formational history of life. Special creation, a term not commonly used until the nineteenth century, is the idea that each species (or some higher level of classification) of plant and animal was independently formed by a divine Craftsman.

According to science historian and Evangelical Christian Richard Aulie, this style of biological theorizing was rooted, not in the belief that the Bible required it, but in the Platonic concept of the fixity of species. In Plato's worldview, earthly species were presumed to be modeled after perfect and eternally unchangeable Ideas or Forms.

Special Creation: A Concept Rejected for Good Reason

Biology long ago abandoned the concepts of unchangeable species and special creation. It did so not as an expression of religious mischief, but simply as an acknowledgement that these concepts failed to give a satisfactory account of many noteworthy observations about closely related species, especially their sequence in time and their distribution over the globe. The concept that did succeed was biological evolution, the transmutation of one species into another by natural processes that are open to investigation.

> If the doctrine of special creation had discernible roots in church history or if it was an unambiguous derivative of biblical exegesis, churches might have reason to gird their loins and do battle. But that is not so. Churches have no need to clothe themselves in this tattered and long-since discarded garment of biology.
> Special creation presupposes a worldview that has roots in Greek antiquity. In conceptual origin and methodology, special creation is a denial of those themes concerning nature and religion that were reaffirmed and passed on to us by the Renaissance and Reformation.
> —Richard P. Aulie, 1983[4]

Special Creation: A Concept Reintroduced without Good Reason

Nonetheless, more than half of the US population today continues to believe that the theory of biological evolution can be tossed out the window and replaced with special creation. But this time the choice is rooted in a contemporary way of reading the early chapters of Genesis, one that is out of touch with major voices in the Judeo-Christian tradition.

Already in the fifth century, Augustine—the bishop who shaped Western theology—argued that finding the literal meaning of Genesis 1–3 (literal in the sense of what it actually means) did not require reading it as a chronicle. Instead, a literal reading of Genesis led Augustine to envision God giving being to a world that was initially formless but gifted with the potentialities (he called them seed principles) for forms that would unfold naturally in the course of time.

Contrary to Augustine's example, however, most Christians today take the biblical phrase "according to their kinds" to be a reference to special creation. It is once again clear from observational evidence, however, that the narratives of Genesis 1 and 2 are not chronicles of what happened and when. It's the familiar problem of "the devil in the details."

One example of devilish detail should be enough: The Genesis 2 story has "Earthling" (Adam, the man, from the Hebrew *adamah*, the ground) appearing prior to shrubs and plants. Observational evidence, on the other hand, clearly demonstrates that modern humans appeared only within the last 100,000 years, hundreds of millions of years after the first appearance of land plants. More headaches for the concordists!

Evolving Creation: A Concept Worth Celebrating

Augustine knew nothing of biological evolution, of course. Neither did he envision one species turning into another in the course of time. But I think he was on to a fruitful approach with his idea of "seed principles" that would come to expression gradually. Here's the essential point: if the world is a Creation, then everything that it is and everything that it is capable of doing is a God-given gift. So, if the world is sufficiently gifted to accomplish something as astounding as evolution, then we should, as Michael Dowd puts it, "thank God for evolution."

There's a very positive way of welcoming the idea that the universe can be viewed as an "evolving Creation." But the reader already knew that. Nonetheless, some very interesting questions remain.

Evolution: A Thought-Provoking Concept

Biological evolution is not the unfolding of a preordained step by-step plan. Evolution's particular pathway was not prescribed in advance; each step in the crafting of new species occurs as a response by existing organisms to the unpredictable circumstances of the moment.

So, did God know that we, the species called *Homo sapiens*, were coming? That seems unlikely to me. It may be tempting to think that the whole purpose of evolution was to bring about our appearance after 13.7 billion years of preparation, but at the moment I see no way to warrant that puffed-up view of the human species. Something like us, perhaps; but exactly us? Unlikely.

But there is still more to ponder. So far, we've been thinking mostly about the evolution of our bodily form. If evolutionary biologists are correct, then the bodies we have inherited from ancestors of long ago are bodies that are loaded with the remnants of what gave them the ability to survive in the challenging environments they encountered in the distant past.

Ah, but it's not only our bodies that evolved. Our brains and the mental processes for which they are equipped are just as much a product of evolutionary development. The brains we inherited from ancestors of long ago have the structures and capabilities that demonstrated survival value in the face of challenges met in the distant past. What our brains are able to do today is what they needed to do to survive yesterday.

So, here's the rub for Earthling (close friends call him *Dusty*):

Earthling's brain is made of the same dust as his body. Earthling's brain, like his body, is optimized for survival. But now Earthling wants to grasp truth, including truth about God. How can Earthling be sure that a brain tuned for survival will be able to tell the difference between comforting illusions and what is true?

There must be a way. Think about it. (More on this in the next study-unit.)

Questions for Further Reflection

1. Why do you think so many people prefer the concept of special creation over evolving creation?
2. Does the idea that we are the products of an evolutionary development in any way diminish or enhance the significance of the human race?
3. Have you ever been inclined to "thank God for evolution"? Why, or why not?
4. How do you tell the difference between comforting illusions and what is true?

Lesson Four: Storied Theology and Truth

[W]idespread belief in God arises from the operation of natural processes of the human mind in ordinary human environments. Belief in God does not amount to anything strange or peculiar; on the contrary, such belief is nearly inevitable.
—Justin Barrett, *Why Would Anyone Believe in God?*[5]

[G]iven our minds' evolved dispositions, the way we live in groups, the way we communicate with other people and the way we produce inferences, it is very likely that we will find in any human group some [set of religious beliefs] whose surface details are specific to a particular group.
—Pascal Boyer, *Religion Explained: The Evolutionary Origins of Religious Thought*[6]

A Question Still on the Table

At the end of the last study-unit, I left readers with a very difficult question to think about. It's a question that naturally pops up when we reflect realistically about how our evolutionary past might have influenced not only how we look, but also how we think. After all, it's not only the human body that has evolved; so has the human mind.

So, here's the rub for Earthling (Dusty): Earthling's brain is made of the same dust as his body. Earthling's brain, like his body, is optimized for survival. But now Earthling wants to grasp truth, including truth about God. How can Earthling be sure that a brain tuned for survival will be able to tell the difference between comforting illusions and what is true?

One Place to Look for Answers

My training in physics and astronomy provides me with a useful pattern for exploring questions, but it's clear that I must look to other disciplines for information and theorizing relevant to the difficult question posed above. The folks I've found most helpful in satisfying my curiosity on these matters are researchers working in a relatively new area called the cognitive science of religion. Cognitive science investigates the mental processes by which we come to know or believe something about the world. Its aim is to craft fruitful and realistic theories about how these brain actions work.

The cognitive science of religion applies its tools for information gathering and theorizing to the phenomenon of religious beliefs and practices. Its goal is not to determine whether any particular religious belief is true or false, but only to find out how humans arrive at religious beliefs and why people participate in religious practices.

The Naturalness of Religion

One thing that the cognitive science folk have learned is that having religious beliefs is a nearly universal human phenomenon: almost everyone holds some sort of religious beliefs. Belief in spirits, gods, or God is as natural and common as hunger. Cognitive science sees this proclivity for religious belief as the by-product of a brain function that was, and continues to be, essential to our survival: the detection of agents, things that have intentions and the ability to carry them out.

Suppose you were walking alone in a remote jungle location. You hear the SNAP of a twig. Startled, you respond intuitively and presume the presence of an agent and initiate evasive action. After all, that snapping sound might signal the presence of a hungry predator. Overreaction is good for survival. If further and more leisurely reflection reveals that the sound was caused by a harmless falling branch, no problem. Under-reaction, however, could be lethal. Failure to detect a prowling lion could mean "you're lunch." Better safe than sorry.

So, the normal human brain is equipped with what Justin Barrett calls a Hypersensitive Agency Detection Device or HADD. Its job is to alert us to agents whose actions may affect us. Now, suppose that a normal human mind, equipped with HADD, formulates a deep question like "Why is there a universe?" HADD's contribution: Maybe our universe is here by action of some remarkable agent.

Perhaps, but the familiar cast of embodied agents (lions, humans, and the like) to whom we might appeal, doesn't seem up to the task of bringing universes into existence. Then why not posit the existence of an un-embodied supernatural agent, a spirit, a Creator, "God"? And while we're at it, why not propose that God is also in charge of establishing universal moral principles and of holding humans accountable for their behavior?

That's the way the human mind works. The rest is history, a history of humanly crafted myths that vary from tribe to tribe and from century to century—storied theology in which the role played by God (or the gods) is deemed essential for understanding the human experience.

But Which Storied Theology Is True?

Having a set of religious beliefs is as natural as natural can be. But the naturalness of religious belief in general tells us nothing about the truth or falsehood of any particular belief. We are back to our question for the day: How can Earthling be sure that a brain tuned for survival will be able to tell the difference between comforting illusions and enduring truths?

Maybe we earthlings should deal with intuitive religious beliefs, the brain's first and automatic responses to religiously significant experiences, in the same way we would deal with a SNAP sound in the jungle. Begin with our brain's first intuition, then turn the matter over to our slower, more rational reflective system and see if our first thoughts hold up. Let intuition have its way initially, but then think about it. Intuition first, evaluation second. Both are important.

Trained as a scientist, I tend to place high value on the rational examination of ideas. Want to find out if some particular religious belief is likely to be true? Good; then run that belief through some basic tests and dare to honor the score. Don't believe something merely because it is emotionally reassuring or because tribal orthodoxy presumes it to be true.

Truth-testing is a lifelong process, but here are the questions that top my list: Is there substantial warrant (reasons, evidence) supporting some particular belief? Does that belief fit comfortably with a seasoned scientific picture of how the world—including the human brain—works? (Science doesn't know everything, of course, but what it does know deserves respect.) Does the fact that you hold this belief enrich your life? Your neighbor's life?

Got beliefs that pass these tests? Good, stick with them until further reflection suggests something different. And by the way, it's wise to be humble about your hold on the truth. Some of what we believe tomorrow may be different from what we believe today. To be alive is to enjoy the unpredictable journey of discovery, not to accept a life sentence of standing at the trailhead.

Questions for Further Reflection
1. Is it important for religious beliefs to be true? If not, what other qualities should beliefs exhibit?
2. Do you test your own beliefs for their truth-value? If so, by what kinds of tests?
3. Is there anything wrong with saying "I don't know" sometimes?
4. What beliefs (true or not) do you now hold that enrich your life? Your neighbor's life?

Final Words

I know that the style of my four "Genesis and Evolution" study-units is very different from the usual "science and Bible in agreement" literature. The concordist approach was explicitly rejected. Biblical inerrancy was never claimed. There were not even any appeals to more modest claims for biblical infallibility on matters of faith and practice.

So, what do these lessons actually represent? Do they represent the thoughts of a person who values a sense of living in the presence of the Sacred and who wishes to respect the Christian Scriptures for what they are, even in the face of science's evolutionary theorizing? Or do they represent the thoughts of a scientist who finds the concepts of cosmic and biological evolution highly credible but sees no warrant for expecting the biblical text to be relevant to the details of that scientific theorizing?

The answer to both of these questions is, Yes, and I hope that this has been clearly communicated in this chapter.

NOTES

1. Source unknown.

2. Grand Rapids: William B. Eerdmans Publishing Company, 1986.

3. Nahum Sarna. 1966. *Understanding Genesis: The Heritage of Biblical Israel*. New York: Schocken Books.

4. Richard P. Aulie. 1983. "Evolution and Creation: Historical Aspects of the Controversy." *Proceedings of the American Philosophical Society*, 127(6): 418–462.

5. Justin L. Barrett. 2004. *Why Would Anyone Believe in God?* Lanham, MD: AltaMira Press. 122.

6. Pascal Boyer. 2001. *Religion Explained: The Evolutionary Origins of Religious Thought.* New York: Basic Books. 321.

Faith and Treason
By Rabbi David E. Kay

Traduttore traditore, goes the somewhat cynical expression: "Translation is treason." The Hebrew Bible has been translated into countless languages and dialects. Some languages have multiple translations. Just glancing at the shelf in my study, I see seven or eight scholarly English translations of the Torah (literally, "instruction," the proper Hebrew name for what is known as the Pentateuch or Five Books of Moses). Which one is correct? All of them and none of them.

The Bible is, first and foremost, literature. Sacred literature, to be sure, but literature nonetheless. As such, it is best and most fully understood in the original.

I've read Dr. Seuss's *Green Eggs and Ham* in Hebrew, and it captures much of the rhythm and whimsy of the English original. But a literal Hebrew translation of the title wouldn't fit the rhyme and meter of the book. What's more, the mention of ham as a desirable and tasty dish that one of the main characters eventually eats and enjoys wouldn't sell well among native Hebrew speakers. The overwhelming majority of them are Jews and Muslims, for whom ham and pork are religious and cultural taboos.

So the Hebrew title of *Green Eggs and Ham* translates back into English as *I Don't Like It, and I'm Not Hungry*. Not quite the same, is it?

So before I can talk about the scriptures of my faith, I have to issue one warning: by dealing with the English translation of Jewish sacred texts, we will have already introduced a layer of inaccuracy. That's really what *traduttore traditore* means: as soon as you move text from its original language into another, you've already corrupted the meaning.

Which brings me to a confession: I believe there's really no such thing as a "literal translation." The highly honored eleventh century French scholar and commentator, Rabbi Shlomo Yitzchaki (known best by the acronym, "Rashi") was the closest thing in Jewish tradition to a literalist. Rashi himself describes his enterprise as providing the reader with *p'shuto shel haMikra*, a phrase which is typically translated (traitorously, of course) as "the plain meaning of the text," but which I think might more precisely be understood as "the unfolding of Scripture." When a passage in the text is convoluted and difficult, Rashi unfolds it and smoothes it out for us.

He does this by finding authoritative Rabbinic interpretations from earlier centuries, and applying them to the problem at hand. But Rashi is also selective. He says up front that there are many valid Rabbinic interpretations which he does *not* choose to bring us. So, is Rashi objective and literal? Not at all. The "plain meaning" is not the literal meaning.

While Jews certainly believe that there are clear and unambiguous statements in our sacred literature, we also recognize that many passages simply do not and cannot have one single meaning. What we do believe is that there is an acceptable *process* of exegesis (interpretation and explanation to draw layers of meaning out of a text) that is authentically Jewish. This is true for other faith traditions that consider the Hebrew Bible as part of their Scripture as well. How else could Judaism and Christianity look at the same passages in the book of Isaiah, for example, and come to radically different conclusions about their theological significance?

What follows is my own bit of treason to the text of the Creation story in the opening chapter of the book of Genesis: my own translation, based on the traditional commentaries that resonate with me, and my own biases and sensitivities.

When God began creating heaven and earth, when the earth was unformed and void, with darkness on the face of the abyss and God's wind sweeping across the surface of the water, God said, "Let there be light"; and there was light. God saw that the light was good, and God made separation between the light and the darkness. God called the light Day, and the darkness Night. Then there was evening and there was morning: one day.

God said, "Let there be a firmament in the midst of the water, and let it make separation between water and water." God made the firmament, and it separated the water above the firmament from the water below the firmament. It was so. God called the firmament Heaven. Then there was evening and there was morning, a second day.

God said, "Let the water below the Heaven be gathered into one place, and let the dry land be seen"; and it was so. God called the dry land Earth, and the gathering of the water God called Seas; and God saw that this was good. Then God said, "Let the Earth sprout vegetation: seed-bearing grasses, fruit trees on the Earth which produce fruit of their kind and whose seed is contained therein"; and it was so. The Earth brought forth vegetation, seed-bearing grasses of each kind, and fruit trees which produce fruit of their kind and whose seed is contained therein. God saw that this was good. Then there was evening and there was morning, a third day.

God said, "Let there be lights in the firmament of Heaven, to make separation between the Day and the Night; they shall be as signs for the set times, the days, and the years. They shall be lights in the firmament of Heaven, to shine upon the Earth"; and it was so. So God made the two great lights, the greater light to dominate the Day and the lesser light to dominate the Night, and the stars. God placed them in the firmament of Heaven to shine upon the Earth, to dominate the Day and the Night, and make separation between the light and the darkness. God saw that this was good. Then there was evening and there was morning, a fourth day.

God said, "Let the waters swarm with swarms of living beings, and birds fly upon the Earth across the firmament of Heaven. God created the great *taninim*1 and every creeping being which swarms the water, according to its kind, and every winged bird, according to its kind; and God saw that this was good. God blessed them, saying, "Be fruitful and multiply, and fill the waters in the Seas, and let the birds multiply on the Earth." Then there was evening and there was morning, a fifth day.

God said, "Let the Earth bring forth living beings, [each] after its kind: cattle and creeping things, and wild beasts, [each] according to its kind." And it was so. God made the wild beast after its kind and cattle after its kind and everything that creeps upon the ground after its kind; and God saw that this was good. Then God said, "Let us make Humans in Our image, after Our likeness." (Genesis 1:1–26)

We moderns frequently make the mistake of dismissing our ancient ancestors as primitives. The Israelites to whom we trace the text of the Torah lived in the Bronze Age, had written language and a body of literature, created ritual and decorative art ranging from painting to pottery to sculpture and metal- and jewel-work, and undertook the engineering feat of designing, building, and periodically transporting their housing, along with livestock and provisions for more than 2,000,000 persons. As part of this seminomadic existence, they also erected (and then occasionally took down and moved) the Tabernacle, the central religious institution.

Once settled in their Promised Land, the Israelites created an infrastructure, some of which still exists today, some 3,000 years later. King Solomon's Temple, palace, and other building projects are the stuff of legend.

Like other ancient cultures, then, the Israelites were far more sophisticated than we usually give them credit for. Passages in the Hebrew Bible which we tend to shrug off as naïve or superstitious (or, on the other end of the spectrum, to take literally and use as refutation of science) were most likely not understood that way by the ancient Israelites.

A case in point is this passage from Deuteronomy 11:

If you will earnestly heed the *mitzvoth* (commandments) I give you this day, to love Adonai your God and serve [God] with all your heart and soul, then I will give timely moisture to your land, the autumn rain and the spring rain, and you shall harvest your grain, your wine, and your oil. I will give grass in your field for your cattle. You shall eat and be satisfied.

Take care lest you let your heart waver, and turn aside, and you serve other gods and bow down to them. Then the ire of Adonai will be upon you, and [God] will stop up the heavens; there shall be no moisture, and the earth will not give its produce. You shall quickly disappear from the good land which Adonai has given you.

Today, we know full well that the weather doesn't depend on how religiously pious people are. We also know all too well that innocent people may suffer the ravages of drought and famine, and wicked people may live in the midst of fair weather and abundance.

If we take the position that the ancient Israelites were primitive and superstitious, we might conclude that God was getting them to toe the line through the time-honored technique of threatening. Being the simple folks we too often take them to be, then, they would have actually believed that when the rains came on time and in the proper amount, they had been good enough to please God, but when there was drought, they had been collectively bad enough to anger God.

Except that's an entirely foolish assumption to make. If anything, my ancient Israelite ancestors were more intimately aware than we are that there was no direct correlation between the relative piety of the community and the weather.

They were largely an agrarian culture, particularly once the Promised Land was settled. For most Americans today, the impact of the weather on farming only shows up in the prices at the supermarket, and even then, we're not very likely to make the connection. But when you're a subsistence farmer, like most of the ancient Israelites, the weather and the agricultural cycle is literally a daily matter of life and death. Too much rain, or rain at the wrong time of year, can be as bad as too little rain. Famine and drought always loom in the background.

As a nation of linked clans with a common ancestor, the Israelites almost certainly knew each other's business. The Tabernacle, and later the Temple in Jerusalem, was a very public place where people brought sacrifices for various sins. The Jerusalem Temple was also the site of three annual pilgrimage festivals, which were supposed to bring all the adult males of the people together. In a nutshell, it was no secret to anybody if the community as a whole had been naughty or nice in a particular year.

So what did the ancient Israelites think in those years when they knew a good number of people had gone astray, yet the rains came and left on time and in their proper amounts, yielding bumper crops of "grain, wine, and oil" and plenty of "grass in the field for the cattle"? Did they say, "Hey! This whole word of God thing must be all wrong!" and abandon the Torah? Obviously not, otherwise Judaism would not have survived.

I can only conclude that they *did not take the text of the Torah literally*, but rather sought the deeper lesson. Here, at Judaism's deepest and most ancient foundations, is established a crucial and fundamental principle in Jewish exegesis: If reality doesn't conform to Scripture, don't assume either is wrong: the problem isn't reality *or* Scripture; the problem is your own understanding of one, the other, or most likely both.

For my ancient Israelite ancestors, God's promises and warnings in Deuteronomy 11 and the evidence of their own experience are not an either-or proposition. Neither one could be denied, though, so the only conclusion they could have reached was that the Torah simply *cannot* be teaching that God uses the weather as direct reward and punishment. Instead, they would have looked beneath the literal meaning of the text to find the lesson that fits both the text and the reality of the world.

That lesson is simply this: Actions have consequences, maybe not right away, but eventually and inevitably. The corollary to that lesson is: Sometimes, seemingly small actions can have far-reaching consequences.

Neither I nor my ancient Israelite ancestors could possibly arrive at such a conclusion if we were literalists. Over a millennium ago, there was a schism in the development of the Judaism we know today. The *Kara'ites* were a stream of Judaism that insisted that proper practice had to be based on a fairly literal reading of the Torah. Their very name comes from the same Hebrew root that gives us a word for Scripture.

For the Kara'ites, the Torah's admonition that "you shall have no fire in your habitations on the Sabbath" literally meant that a fire could not be burning in a Jewish home from before sundown every Friday until after dark every Saturday. While the Rabbinic Jewish tradition, which has guided Judaism since the destruction of the Second Jerusalem Temple, allows for a fire to be kindled before sundown on Friday and to burn throughout the night to provide heat and light, Kara'ites apparently sat in the cold and dark every Sabbath eve.

The Rabbinic interpretation of the restriction on fire during the Sabbath is clearly not a literal one, but it does make both logical and theological sense. In this way, these ancient Sages of Judaism did not invent interpretations out of convenience. Rather, they found ways to understand sacred text that were both reverent and relevant. In Rabbinic parlance, this is called *peirush* ("interpretation;" but more literally, if we may, "to separate out [a layer of meaning]").

Applying this logical/theological approach to the Creation narrative yields profound results. Almost immediately, a literalist reading of the text breaks down:

When God began creating heaven and earth, when the earth was unformed and void, with darkness on the face of the abyss and God's wind sweeping across the surface of the water, God said, "Let there be light"; and there was light.

The first question the literalist must ask is, "Where did the darkness come from?" If God is indeed the Creator of all, it could not have existed prior to Creation! My English translation of the original Hebrew helps. Rather than the King James Version type of rendering—"In the beginning, God created the heaven and the earth"—this translation reflects the subtlety of the Hebrew grammar, letting us know that the process of Creation *was already underway* when we pick up the story with the creation of light. The "unformed and void" earth, darkness, and "the abyss" had already been made.

But the literalist reading's narrow escape is only temporary:

God saw that the light was good, and God made separation between the light and the darkness. God called the light Day, and the darkness Night. Then there was evening and there was morning: one day.

See the problem here? The literalist must understand "evening," "morning," and "day" in the same way they are used today *and* elsewhere in the Bible. That's particularly difficult, since "evening" in this context would therefore require the setting of the sun, something which won't even exist until the fourth "day" of the Creation story.

Complicating this is the literalist assumption that "one day"—in Hebrew, the ordinal "one" is used rather than the cardinal "first"—is twenty-four hours. There is no internal definition of the length of a day until much later in the Torah, when it is described as being from sundown to sundown. Since there has never been a sunset at this point in the Creation narrative, it's impossible to attest to the length of this "one day."

There is an additional problem with using a twenty-four-hour day here, one that is wholly theological and entirely ironic. Literalist readings of the Bible are typically justified by claiming to retain authenticity and preserve the original meaning. However, the measuring of time is a distinctly *human* artifact. God does not measure time by hours or days or even years. God is timeless. Psalm 90:4 describes this poetically:

For a thousand years in Your eyes is like a yesterday which has passed

Or as a watch in the night.

From the divine perspective, a thousand years is the equivalent of a day or even of a few hours ("a watch in the night"). Whose time are we operating on in the Creation narrative, the Creator's or the created's?

But there is another objection to literalist reading of the Hebrew Bible that, by itself, should be sufficient: literal reading of the text strips it of its inherent beauty and meaning. Whether one believes that the Hebrew Bible represents the explicit word of God, or that it is a compilation of the work of multiple human authors and redactors over a period of centuries (or anything in between), it is clearly intended to be a work of the utmost profundity and subtlety. One simply cannot grasp the many layers of meaning in a literary work of this magnitude by taking it entirely at face value.

Turn It and Turn It

In the Jewish tradition, we read through the entirety of the Torah, the Five Books of Moses, each year, in a cycle of consecutive weekly portions. In an adult lifetime, a Jew can expect to hear the entire primary sacred text of his or her faith read aloud over fifty times. Yet, as anyone who rereads a favorite novel or repeatedly watches a favorite movie dozens of times over the years knows, there is always something new to be learned, some new gem to discover, some new insight to be gained.

"Turn it and turn it," our ancient Sages, of blessed memory, say of the Torah, "for everything is in it." Like an intricate jewel, all of its beauty cannot be perceived from a single perspective. It's not that a literal reading of the text is necessarily wrong (although often it is), but it is virtually always inadequate, and therefore entirely misleading.

Any person of faith would agree that his or her sacred text is written purposefully and deliberately. As a result, the use of certain literary structures or motifs in that text is not random or accidental. We're not talking about the so-called "Bible codes" here, but rather clear use of devices like foreshadowing, dramatic irony, and parallelism.

This last literary device, parallelism, is employed brilliantly and subtly in the Creation narrative in Genesis. First, a quick summary of the works of Creation on each of the "days."

Day 1 – Light/darkness
Day 2 – Firmament/separation of waters "above" and "below"
Day 3 – Dry land/definition of seas/land vegetation
Day 4 – Sun, moon, stars
Day 5 – Sea creatures/birds
Day 6 – Land animals/human beings

A literal reading misses the parallelism here, the correlation between Days 1 and 4, 2 and 5, and 3 and 6:

This day	Correlates to this day
Day 1: Light/dark (Day/Night)	Day 4: Sun, moon, stars
Day 2: Sky/separate water "above" and "below"	Day 5: Sea creatures, birds
Day 3: Dry land/boundary of seas/land plants	Day 6: Land animals, human beings

Notice how the first element in each pair establishes boundaries and separates the pairs of complementary opposites that form the "raw material" or habitat for the second element. The first recorded act of divine Creation, the calling into being of light on Day 1, is necessary to the understanding and existence of "the greater lights" and the "lesser lights" on Day 4. Likewise, the separation of light and darkness, and their naming as Day and Night, are necessary for "the greater light to dominate the Day, and the lesser light to dominate the Night."

Similarly, the primordial watery chaos that already exists when Genesis picks up the story ("God's wind [was] sweeping across the face of the water") is separated into "the water above" and "the water below" by means of a firmament on Day 2. This separation barrier between upper and lower water sources is called Heaven, a necessary precursor to the creation of birds on Day 5, just as "the water below" is a necessary precursor to the creation of sea creatures.

Finally, the separation of water and dry land is necessary for the emergence of terrestrial vegetation on Day 3, and both events are needed to create land animals and human beings, who are given all those growing things as food on Day 6.

Two aspects of this deeper analysis of the Creation story are startling in their compatibility with modern scientific understanding of the earth's natural history. First, there is the fact that life on earth begins in the seas, and that more complex organisms appear progressively later in the process. Second, the parallel day pairs show a progression from non-differentiation to differentiation, from simple and non-specific to more complex and specialized.

This is a rather precise description of the process of *speciation*, the development and divergence of different species of plants and animals.

Speciation was the very thing which bothered Charles Darwin so much about William Paley's "Argument from Design," the dominant theory of natural history in his day. If all of nature came into being in a sort of supernatural architecture, why have so many different species?

Certainly, one could argue that "variety is the spice of life," and having several different species of hummingbird is simply a divine enhancement of the beauty of the natural world. However, what Darwin saw as totally inconsistent with the Argument from Design was why species would go extinct or new species arise. Thus, in his landmark book, *The Origin of Species and the Descent of Man*, Darwin would introduce his concept of natural selection as the engine that drives the emergence, development, and extinction of types of living things.

If Darwin had set out to challenge the validity of the Biblical account of Creation, he would have chosen a different title for his book. Instead, he chose one which points to the problem he endeavors to solve: that *within nature*, there is an observable phenomenon of species appearing and disappearing. In *The Origin of Species*, Darwin lays out a theory that identifies and describes this natural process, and explores how human beings might fit in such a framework.

This is precisely what our analysis of the Creation narrative does as well. It places the process of speciation, the specialization and diversification of species, squarely within the divine plan. Thus, evolution is not only compatible with the book of Genesis, some of its basic principles are contained within it.

In truth, this should come as absolutely no surprise to us. In the central prayer of our weekday liturgy, Jews pray:

You grace a human being with intellect, and teach a person understanding; through You we are graced with intellect, understanding, and enlightenment. You are praised, *Adonai*, the One Who graces with intellect.

Human intelligence, insight, understanding and wisdom are divine gifts. To refuse to apply these, to deny the knowledge and deeper grasp of God's Creation that arise from these, would be at best ungrateful and at worst, a rejection of God.

Likewise, any attempt to "prove" the Bible denies its primary function as a sacred text, a document of and for the faithful. It is a weak and precarious faith that cannot tolerate a challenge to its assumptions. At the end of the day, it is not empirical evidence, but rather belief that sustains the faith of a believer. The pressing need to force reality to fit one's particular understanding of one's sacred text is an act of desperation, not of piety.

For example, the Torah is quite clear on the rules of evidence for capital offenses. No person can incur a death penalty unless there is corroborating testimony from at least two eyewitnesses. The Rabbis of the Talmud further clarified and qualified these rules of testimony, citing other Biblical sources, to require that the witnesses not only saw the person about to commit the capital offense, but warned him or her that committing the act would incur a death penalty, then heard the perpetrator state explicitly that he or she knew this, didn't care about the consequences, and intended to willfully commit the act anyway. Finally, the eyewitnesses had to actually see the capital offense committed.

By this traditional Jewish standard, very few, if any, of the some 5,000 executions carried out by the civilian courts in our country in the last century should have happened. As an observant and committed Jew, I can therefore oppose the death penalty on religious grounds. But I can't expect that capital cases tried in civilian courts will adhere to the parameters the Torah and Rabbinic law require.

In fact, if I were charged with a capital crime in those same civilian courts, I should not expect that those courts' failure to adhere to Biblical rules of evidence and testimony would guarantee my never being executed. The reality of the legal system does not conform to my system of belief, but that does not invalidate either the civilian courts' authority or my faith tradition.

Perhaps it's an historical and cultural thing with us Jews. As a people and a faith tradition, we have been under relentless attack for millennia. We've long ago learned to roll with the punches, to maintain our faith within our own communities, and to let other faith traditions do likewise. We embrace not only diversity but paradox itself. To be honest, we *thrive* on paradox. Our deepest and oldest roots are in the East, where logic need not flow in the straight line that so much of Western culture demands.

So, when Judaism is presented with scientific theory that gives at least the appearance of contradicting Biblical text, Judaism doesn't tend to react to it as an either/or proposition. The Talmud, the core Rabbinic text of our tradition, is based on the assumption that once a question has been argued and analyzed thoroughly, it is not always necessary to arrive at a single authoritative conclusion.

Think of that scene in *Fiddler on the Roof*, where a fellow makes a point and Tevye comments, "He's right." When another fellow makes exactly the opposite point, Tevye again remarks, "He's right." Another bystander says, "He's right and he's right. They can't *both* be right!" Tevye considers this a moment, then replies, "You know, you are *also* right."

Or, as the Talmud itself puts it, after two schools of thought present equally persuasive arguments for their differing position, *Eilu v'eilu div'rei Elohim hayyim*: "Both of these are the words of the living God!"

So even if I didn't see harmony between the text of the Torah and the insights of Darwin's theories—and I most certainly do see that harmony—I would still have no opposition to evolution on religious grounds. Science is the exercise of our God-given intellectual abilities, and what it produces, assuming that it has been done properly and integrally, is a part of divine revelation too.

A few years ago, a rabbinic colleague of mine caused a bit of a stir when he gave a sermon during Passover in which he observed that there is no archeological evidence that the Israelites were ever enslaved in Egypt, let alone that they left *en masse*.

"Rabbi Claims Exodus Never Happened," screamed the headlines.

Of course, he had said no such thing. Rather, he had repeated a fact that archeologists and Bible scholars have known for decades. There *is* no archeological evidence to support the Torah's claim that there was a captive population of what must have been at least two million Israelites living in Egypt some 3,300 years ago, and that all of them, plus their flocks and herds, and a "mixed multitude" of non-Israelites, picked up and left one night.

So what's the point of bringing up this scientific reality, if not to challenge the Bible's account and undermine the congregation's faith? The point is simply *Eilu v'eilu divrei Elohim hayyim*. One need not reject the truth of one in order to embrace belief in the other.

You see, the primary purpose of the Exodus story is not to record historical fact. It is our people's *historiography*, the literary record of our history. George Washington throwing a dollar across the Potomac (a far more significant sum of money to toss away in those days than it is today, by the way) or telling his father that he chopped down the cherry tree have long ago been dismissed as fabrications. Yet they are much more than folklore: they are an integral part of American culture. We assign these noble attributes of strength and honesty to "the father of our country" because we believe that these are founding principles of our nation. If America is strong and true, then its first President must have been so as well. In this way, it doesn't matter whether the dollar-across-the-Potomac or cherry tree stories are *factually* true: they are true in a sense that transcends factuality.

Likewise, the historiography of the Exodus as recorded in the Torah transcends the archeological evidence, or lack thereof, to the contrary. It doesn't matter if science can't or doesn't confirm what's written there, any more than it matters if what's written there can or does confirm science. If it *did* matter, we'd be back to Galileo being forced, under pain of excommunication and death, to recant his observations that the earth moves around the sun.

Yet, for all the discussion and debate, there is an extremely important element that is all but overlooked. It is really this comparatively small and quiet point that guides me most as both scientist and Jew:

None of us should have the arrogance to declare that we know for a fact how the universe works.

The one who truly understands science will readily admit that we absolutely do *not* know, that the sum total of all our brilliance and discoveries and insights is the most miniscule fraction of what there is to know. How much more so should this be true for the person of faith, who believes that this vast body of "what there is to know" is, by definition, an infinitesimal fraction of an eternal, all-present and omniscient God.

When I was an undergraduate, earning my degree in the life sciences, I was required to take biochemistry. This remarkable course had the goal of teaching us the chemical pathways and reactions of central metabolism, that crucial process which goes on in every somatic cell of our bodies and results in producing the energy we need to live. To understand central metabolism is to understand how nutrients, air and water are processed at the most basic microscopic level in the human body, producing ATP (adenosine triphosphate), the basic energy units of life.

Studying for my final exam, which essentially meant being able to recall and reconstruct from memory the many interwoven pathways and reactions, along with the chemical structure of most of their components, I locked myself in a classroom in the university's Foreign Language Building. This room had blackboards on three of its four walls. Not only that, they were motorized two-level blackboards. You could fill one, push the button, send it up, and then continue writing on the one behind (and now also below) it.

Several hours later, I had filled both levels of blackboards on two adjoining walls with the intricate details of central metabolism. Impressed with the work of my hands, I signed and dated it, and prepared to head home for a few well-earned hours of sleep for the exam the next morning. As I stood at the door, with my hand on the light switch, I looked back one last time to admire my handiwork. And then it hit me.

My God! I thought, really meaning that expression in its most precise and personal sense, for a change. *If just one of these reactions fails, you're dead.*

There I was, mere weeks away from being awarded my Bachelor of Science from the Department of Ecology, Ethology (animal behavior), and Evolution, and this impressive display of scientific evidence had led me to this conclusion: No system this complex, this elegant, this intricate, and this incredibly efficient and reliable could have come into being totally at random.

This is exactly the sort of flash of insight that leads some to conclude that evolution must therefore be wrong and some version of "intelligent design" must be right. Yet mine was quite the opposite experience. This was and remains one of the most deeply spiritual moments of my life. It was one of those rare and wonderful instants when the absolute certainty of the Divine was abundantly and irrefutably clear. And it came because of my mastery of a single narrow slice of one area of *scientific* study.

What else could I possibly conclude from such an experience, except that science and theology are not contradictory—or worse, competitive—means of explaining the world? Rather, they are two intimately intertwined ways in which human beings endeavor to grasp the infinite reality of Creation.

From the perspective of Judaism, there can never really be a clash between sincere, legitimate, and integral science and a sincere, legitimate, and integral reading of the Hebrew Bible. Both are human intellectual processes, and therefore divinely given and to be cherished and used to the fullest. The Hebrew Bible's literary value does not make it "secular," nor does the inherent spirituality of scientific insight make science "religious." Such distinctions unfairly and inaccurately narrow our understanding of both, limiting our use of the God-given gift of intellect, and denying us the fullest experience of the reality of the divine.

To be fair, there are those streams within Judaism, small minority that they may be, that have a fundamental theological problem with evolution. These streams do not reject science. On the contrary, they consider all human knowledge to be subsumed within the rubric of "Torah" in its broadest sense of "divine instruction." Like me, Jews in these more fundamentalist streams believe that science and Scripture are both explored and understood through the gift of human intellect.

So where's the theological problem? It has to do with the age old philosophical riddle of whether a perfect God can create an imperfect creation. For this tiny and marginal group within the Jewish world, saying that *any* species or individual adapts or changes over time suggests that God's Creation is imperfect and therefore casts doubt on the perfection of God.

Making matters worse, this fundamentalist stream of Judaism makes a very literal count of years from the genealogies of the Hebrew Bible, concluding that the universe is several thousand years old, rather than the billions of years that science holds it to be.

Clearly, human remains dating back tens of thousands of years don't jibe with such a world-view. And dinosaur bones dating back millions of years are even more of an issue. Yet, in the typically Jewish way I've described, even these literalist or fundamentalist Jews don't dispute the reality or accuracy of carbon dating and other scientific tools. Instead, they maintain that the world *was* created less than 6,000 years ago, but with million-year-old dinosaur bones and 10,000-plus-year-old human remains *already in it*.

There is no arguing with this sort of self-contained logic. It assumes its conclusions are absolutely correct, and adapts the evidence to concur with those conclusions. As an exercise in faith, it's perfectly acceptable. But it's not science. Science, done well and properly, adapts its conclusions to reflect the evidence.

But, once again, this does not make science the opposite of religion. Both are actually based on the same fundamental belief of the perfection of the natural world, and both attempt to find explanations of the perceived imperfections within that world. Darwin was never looking to refute or replace the existence of God or the validity of Scripture. Darwin sought an intrinsic process, a natural, reliable mechanism *within* God's Creation, that would help us understand that what appeared imperfect and random (the appearance, disappearance, proliferation, and diversification of species) in fact was perfectly orderly.

Likewise, Scripture does not seek to refute or replace science, but rather places human beings into the context of the natural world. The book of Genesis may consider humans the crown of Creation, but, as such, we are very clearly *part* of that Creation.

The Garden of Eden is synonymous with "paradise," a place of perfection, harmony and balance. Different faith traditions read the Garden of Eden story in their own ways, but one thing remains consistent: it didn't start going badly for human beings until after they broke from the divinely established patterns of nature.

Again, Judaism has the advantage of reading this story in the original Hebrew. Minus the treason of translation, the Garden of Eden narrative is not a "fall from grace" or "original sin," but an example of the inevitable result of the exercise of free will by imperfect beings. Blessed with intellect, curiosity and the ability to make choices, human beings have a terribly hard time accepting the fact that they are a part of the natural world. As a result, we consistently find ourselves at odds with it, laboring to grow food, to propagate our species, to survive.

The Mark of Cain

Human evolution is the great bugaboo in the dialogue between science and religion. Even where people of faith can accept the notion that animals and plants might adapt and evolve over time, they are often still uncomfortable with the thought of humanity emerging from ancestors who were decidedly non-human.

Our earlier literary analysis of the parallelism in Genesis 1 strongly suggests that the Torah has a basic concept strikingly similar to Darwin's. But that very same text makes a marked distinction between the appearance of human beings and the appearance of virtually everything else in the universe. While light and darkness, water and land, plants and sea creatures, animals and birds all come into being by divine decree ("Let there be . . . / And there was . . ."), humans have a very different origin:

Adonai, God, formed the Human from the dust of the earth, and blew into its nostrils the breath of life; thus the Human became a living being. (Genesis 2:7)

Of all the myriad elements of God's Creation, then, only human beings come into existence by direct divine action. To create humans, God does not decree, God forms and breathes life into the original model.

Reconciling this unique creative process with evolutionary theory is a much more daunting task. Our literary analysis of the Creation narrative doesn't help us much. In fact, it appears only to make things more difficult. There is no parallelism for the creation of humans.

Of course, we might expect that. This is, after all, a moral and ethical guidebook for humans. If you want to make the point that we, out of all creatures on earth, have the unique ability to make free choices, and that there are better and worse ways of exercising that ability, you'd want to make it from the very beginning of our existence.

So at least one of the messages in the Bible's description of the creation of humanity is that we are unique and unparalleled, and that can be a good thing or not, depending on how we choose to apply it. Humans are capable of achievements and nobility unparalleled in the rest of the world. But we're also capable of unparalleled destructiveness and wickedness.

The inherent nature of human free will is an integral part of the Creation narrative. The first human children, Cain and Abel, grow up and offer sacrifices to God. The Hebrew of the passage is somewhat difficult, but the gist is that Abel's sacrifice is acceptable while Cain's is not. Cain is distraught and a little resentful, so God warns him:

Surely, if you do right there is uplift, but if you do not do right sin crouches at the door! Its urge is toward you, yet you can be its master. (Genesis 4:6–7)

We don't get the details of what happens next, but the outcome is the infamous first murder. Somewhat surprisingly, Cain is not sentenced to death, but rather to a sort of exile:

Then [God] said, "What have you done? The voice of your brother's blood cries out to Me from the ground! So now you shall be more cursed than the ground which opened its mouth to take your brother's blood from your hand. When you work the soil, it shall no longer yield its strength to you: you shall be a ceaseless wanderer on the earth." (Genesis 4:10–12)

Even with God's lenient and merciful response to his crime, Cain's reaction is utter despair:

Cain said to Adonai, "My punishment is too great to bear! Since you have banished me this day from the soil and I must avoid Your presence and be a ceaseless wanderer on the earth, then anyone who meets me may kill me!" (Genesis 4:13–14)

So God puts Cain under divine protection, promising "if anyone kills Cain, sevenfold vengeance shall be taken on him." To seal the agreement, God "put a mark on Cain, lest anyone who meet him should kill him."

Which leaves us with a most perplexing question: who are all these people Cain is worried about? Since Abel is dead, aren't Cain and his parents, Adam and Eve, the only human beings left? And if Cain is being sent away to wander, he won't be anywhere near them.

The traditional commentaries on the Hebrew Bible offer two ways out of this dilemma. This first says that Cain is talking about future siblings, nieces and nephews, or grand-nieces and grandnephews, out to avenge the murder of their kinsman. Of course, this requires us to accept that Cain, who didn't even consider the immediate consequences of his own actions, is mortally afraid of people who aren't even born yet and who won't be a threat for many years to come.

Rashi, the eleventh-century rabbi, scholar, and commentator mentioned earlier, draws on ancient Rabbinic tradition to offer the other, quite creative solution to the problem:

"Anyone who meets me may kill me." [Meaning] the beasts and the wild animals; but [other] human beings did not yet exist, that he should fear them, only his father and mother, and he did not fear they would kill him. Rather he said, "Until now, the fear of me was upon all the wild animals, as it is written (Genesis 9:2), *The fear of you [shall be upon every beast]*, but now, on account of this transgression, the wild animals will no longer fear me and they will kill me." Immediately, *Adonai placed a sign upon Cain* (Genesis 4:15) [that is, God] restored the fear of him upon the wild animals.

As clever as that sounds, there's a large fly in the logical ointment: the bit about the fear of humans being on every beast and wild animal doesn't happen until after the Great Flood, some ten generations later than when Cain is speaking here.

A literal reading of the Biblical origin of human beings is hopelessly ambiguous. We haven't even touched on the fact that a literal reading of Genesis 2 tells a different version of the entire Creation story, perhaps even placing humans in the Garden of Eden *before* the animals. No matter what your theology, your ideology, your politics, or your faith tradition, the only way to iron out the difficulties in this text is through some sort of interpretation.

From the Jewish perspective, this means always keeping in mind that the very word "Torah" means "instruction." In its reading of the Torah, the primary question for Judaism is not so much "What does it mean?" as "What does it come to teach us?" The point of the Creation narrative, including the creation of human beings, is not to record the precise events, exactly as they happened and in the exact order they happened. In fact, the ancient Rabbis warn against attempting that very thing. "The works of the Beginning," as it is called in Hebrew, could only have been accomplished by God, and therefore can only truly be understood by God.

Instead, we must draw moral and ethical imperatives from the Creation story. The Sages of the Talmud even ask why a book of instruction should include the Creation story at all: wouldn't it be more reasonable to cut right to the chase and start with the first commandment given specifically to the Israelites? Thus, they conclude, there must be important lessons in the Creation story. And since those lessons are from a time before Abraham and the covenant with his descendants, they must be directed to all of humankind.

One of those universal lessons is that we are all descended from a common ancestor pair. The moral point here is that no human being can claim superiority over another. We're all literally part of the same family.

All of humanity descending from a common ancestor pair is also, by the way, precisely what evolution predicts.

At some point in the gradual process of natural selection, a breeding pair produces offspring that have a genetic configuration significantly different from their parents' generation and most, if not all, of their own generation, different enough that they can no longer interbreed successfully. This is a scientific line in the sand for separating similar-looking species. A dog and a wolf can produce pups that can themselves produce more dog-wolf hybrid pups. A donkey and a horse, by contrast, produce a mule. A big, strong, strapping animal to be sure, but completely unfit, in terms of evolution. A mule is sterile, incapable of reproducing. Donkeys and horses may look very similar, but they have diverged enough as individual species that the gap can no longer be bridged by cross breeding.[2]

According to the current understanding of human evolution, around the same time horses and donkeys were diverging into separate species, "proto-humans" given the genus name *Australopithecus* roamed the earth. *Australopithecus* walked on two legs, and their teeth, feet, and hands are strikingly human-like.

In the late Pliocene Era, about 2.5 million years ago or so, the first version of the genus *Homo* diverged from *Australopithecus*: *Homo habilis*. *Homo erectus* evolved from, and eventually replaced, *Homo habilis*, which in turn gave rise to and was replaced by *Homo neanderthalensis*.

By this time, roughly 50,000 years ago or so, the emerging humans were using tools and creating useful objects from existing materials. There is even some slight evidence to suggest the creation of ritual objects, the possible origin of what we now call art.

Homo neanderthalensis gave rise to another new species, the one we know best: *Homo sapiens*, the modern human. The two species are thought to have co-existed for thousands of years, until *Homo neanderthalensis* finally went extinct worldwide. There appear to have been other species in the genus *Homo* that diverged from these lines over the millennia, "cousins" of *Homo sapiens*, rather than direct descendants.

Overall, human evolutionary theory posits at least eight successive and progressive species over some three million years, gradually making the transition from an early, upright-walking proto-human with a brain about a third of the size of ours, to the dawn of what we know as human civilization. As the new and better-adapted species flourished, the species from which it diverged was gradually out-competed and went extinct.

This is a good opportunity to further debunk the myth that evolution says monkeys evolve into people. Monkeys had actually *diverged* from the evolutionary line that leads to humans several million years earlier than genus *Homo*. In fact, by the time *Australopithecus* stood upright, monkeys were already an entirely separate species.

Our closest living relatives are chimpanzees. Humans and chimps share some 95 percent of DNA, suggesting they diverged from their common evolutionary line recently. But that's "recently" in evolutionary time: millions of years. If evolution required some sort of inevitable march from ape to human, we wouldn't talk about a thousand chimps with typewriters being able to produce the works of Shakespeare at random. Chimps would have had enough time to have their own Shakespeare by now.

Armed with this basic understanding of human evolution, let's return to Cain's fearful cry to God that his punishment for murder is too great because "any who meet me will kill me." Recall that this punishment strikes us as fairly lenient: he's to be a failure as a farmer, and must wander the earth to find his sustenance. In literary terms, this is called an *origin story*. It explains the existence of the nomadic peoples of the ancient Near East.

We tend to romanticize the nomadic life, but it was and is actually fraught with danger. Without a place to call home, nomads run the constant risk of crossing into the land and provoking the wrath of those who have staked out permanent territories.

Cain doesn't have a tribe or a clan or even another family member to protect him or to come to his defense as he wanders. If a nomadic tribe in the ancient Near East was at risk, a single nomadic individual would have a very short life expectancy indeed. Understood this way, Cain's punishment can be seen as a sort of death penalty after all.

But wait. The whole problem with this text is that Cain could already account for all the other humans in the world, his parents, and they were not a threat. Perhaps Cain is worried about crossing into the hunting territories of some wild animal? No, that's the explanation Rashi brought, and we found lacking.

So if the "anyone" Cain is afraid of is not a human or a nonhuman, what could it possibly be? Well, what if it were a *prehuman*?

Could we possibly understand Adam and Eve and Cain and Abel to be the first fully human family, and Cain's fear of being sent out alone a justifiable terror of the much more primitive and potentially dangerous *Homo neanderthalensis*? Admittedly, there is nothing in the text that compels us to reach this rather radical conclusion. Yet, somewhat surprisingly, any but a narrowly literal reading of the narrative can accommodate it.

Once again, though, a precise harmonizing of scientific theory and Biblical text is simply not necessary to establish the validity of either. Each addresses the question of human origins in its own individual context and with its own individual language.

The Torah calls the primordial human pair *Adam* ("human") and *Havah* ("life"; in English, Eve). Their first child is *Kayin*, (Cain) from the Hebrew root meaning "to acquire" or "to obtain," since Eve declares, "I have obtained (another) human from God!"

Their second child is called *Havel* (Abel), meaning "vapor" or "insubstantial," an indication that he will disappear without reproducing. Here is yet another literary device in the Torah: *nomen omen* ("the name is the sign"), the naming of characters according to what they will do in the story.

The most recent research in human evolution uses *mitochondrial DNA* (mitDNA)[3] to trace linkages between human populations and mathematically project their origins and common ancestors. This model points to a common matrilineal (mother-to-daughter inheritance) ancestor for all humans, who lived in Africa some 150,000 years ago.

There was only one name researchers could see fit to call her: Eve.

And why not? Researchers like Dr. Allan Wilson—credited with coining the name—and others aren't claiming that "Mitochondrial Eve" is the Eve of the Garden of Eden. There certainly would have to have been other human men and women at the time Mitochondrial Eve lived. The difference is that while these other early humans *might* still have *some* descendants today, Mitochondrial Eve's mitDNA has been passed down from mother to offspring to *every* human being alive today.[4] Neither are researchers claiming that Mitochondrial Eve is the most recent common ancestor (MRCA) for all human beings. Statistical models suggest our

MRCA[5] lived perhaps 4,000 years ago. Ironically enough, this fits well with what some literalists claim was the time of Biblical Adam and Eve.

Mitochondrial Eve's name wasn't chosen as some sort of anti-Biblical statement, though. She is, literally speaking, the mother of us all, and her name is homage to Genesis 3:20:

The human called his woman's name *Havah* (Eve), because she was the mother of all the living.

But aren't we really forcing the issue here? After all, we've said explicitly that Mitochondrial Eve is not the Eve of the Bible, that other humans lived with and before her, and that at least some of us are descended from those other humans. What's more, Mitochondrial Eve's male counterpart, Y-chromosomal Adam, whose sex-determining chromosome is carried by all current males, is projected to have lived at least 70,000 years after her.

It would seem that we've really done nothing but demonstrate the disparity between the Bible and science, where the origin of human beings is concerned.

In fact, what we've done is used human evolutionary genetics to confirm that the traditional Jewish explanation for why the Creation narrative and the origin of human beings is necessary to include in a book called "Instruction" (Torah) at all.

The fundamental moral lesson for all humanity to be learned from Mitochondrial Eve, Y-chromosome Adam, and our MRCA is no different than the one brought forward by the medieval Jewish commentator, quoting the Rabbis of the Talmud from a millennium before that: we are all literally part of the same human family, and none of us can say "My ancestors were greater than yours."

NOTES

1. Often translated as "sea-monsters," the precise meaning of this Biblical Hebrew word is uncertain. In modern Hebrew, it means "crocodiles," an extension of the assumed Biblical meaning.

2. Technically, a "mule" is any sterile offspring of two different species. In popular usage, a mule is the offspring of a male donkey and a female horse. The offspring of a female donkey and a male horse is a "hinny." In hundreds of years of recorded history of mules and hinnies bred by humans, there have been sixty or so cases of female mules being successfully bred with male horses. There are no recorded cases of male mules or hinnies siring offspring.

3. mitDNA is different from nuclear DNA. Children receive equal amounts of nuclear DNA from each parent. mitDNA is passed only from the mother to offspring, both male and female. However, male children

do not pass it on to their own offspring.

4. See A. C. Wilson, *et. al.* 1985. "Mitochondrial DNA and two perspectives on evolutionary genetics." *Biological Journal of the Linnean Society*, 26:375–400.

5. See D. L. T. Rohde, S Olson, J. T. Chang. 2004. "Modeling the recent common ancestry of all living humans." *Nature* 431: 562–566.

The Universe: A Written Scroll and a Sign
By T.O. Shanavas

All religions and science share certain common characteristics. They have metaphysical commitments. Philosophers use the term "metaphysics" to refer to the general vision of reality that one holds to be true. Science's metaphysical commitments are based on the faith that the five senses are the only portals of knowledge; all wisdom comes from the material world; scientific methodology is the only way to verify truth; and the universe is intelligible. On the other hand, the religion of Islam is based upon faith in a God who shares His wisdom with His human creatures through His revelations.

Both religion and science explain reality based on evidence obtained by different schemes of enquiry. Religion has access to thinking, reasoning, or other mental activity as well as divine revelation, while science has access to only reason and sensual knowledge arrived at empirically. Practitioners of science accept freely that their conclusions and theories are uncertain truths, even though these are based on repeated experiments and observation. For religions, what appear as "laws of nature" are reflections of Divine Wisdom and Will. For science, facts of nature are phenomena that are to be studied and explained either mathematically or descriptively, and the explanations are tested again and again against nature. They do not refer to a higher order of reality. For religion, phenomena of nature are the symbols or signs of God, who is the highest order of reality.

The Qur'an and the physical universe are twin manifestations of the divine act of Self-revelation. Viewed as a text, the universe is a "written scroll" — "The Day when We shall roll up the heavens as a recorder rolleth up a written scroll." (Qur'an 21:104)[1] — with information that must be read according to its meaning. The Qur'an is the counterpart of the physical universe, a text in human vernacular that bids us to explore and coexist with the universe without damaging it. This divine proposal to humans comes through the following verse:

The sun and the moon pursue their scheduled courses on their axis according to a fixed reckoning. And the stem-less plants and the trees humbly submit to His will; and He raised the heaven high and set up the [law of] harmony and balance; [He explains this to you] that you should not violate the [law of] harmony and balance. Hold balance with justice [giving everyone his due avoiding extremes] and do not disturb the [law of] harmony in the least. (Qur'an 55:5–9) [2]

The Qur'anic verses are called *ayahs*, and similarly, the Qur'an describes phenomena of nature as divine *ayahs*. The earth, sky, mountains, stars, oceans and the ships that float upon them, and all the living creatures in this universe are ayahs. The Qur'an states:

It is He who made the earth a bed for you and has threaded it with pathways for you. He sends down rain from the clouds. We bring forth by means of this [water] pairs of vegetation of diverse kinds. [So that you may] eat it and pasture your cattle [upon it]. Verily, in all this there are signs (ayahs) for the people possessing sound reason. (Qur'an 20:53–54)[3]

Truly in the creation of the heavens and the earth, and in the alternation of the night and the day are signs (ayahs) for those who have acumen, who utter [the name of] God, standing, and sitting and on their sides, and ponder over the creation of the heavens and the earth, [saying], 'Our Lord, You have not created these in futility.' (Qur'an 3:190–191)[4]

Therefore, both the Qur'an and the phenomena of nature are direct communications and guidance from God to the human species. The Qur'an urges its believers "to reflect" on the creation because it is "not created in vain."

Harmony between the Qur'an and Nature

For Muslims, uncorrupted religion emanating from the Qur'an and uncorrupted science derived from nature cannot conflict with each other because God is the author of the Qur'an and of nature. The Qur'an instructs humankind: "Say: 'Travel in the earth and see how He makes the first creation, then Allah creates the later creation. Surely Allah is Possessor of power over all things.' " (Qur'an 29:20)[5] The verse implies that the divine process of creation and its products are comprehensible, and all necessary tools for humans to study the universe are provided on the earth. If God told humans one thing and gave the physical evidence for another on the earth, this would do the opposite of proving His existence. Therefore, the history of the origin of life and its evolution, based upon hard data gathered from the earth by humans, cannot conflict with the divine. However, if there is conflict between the interpretation of vernacular and material revelations from God, it is due to deficiencies in human understanding of the two revelations. Therefore, the conflict arises out of our interpretations, not from the pure religion itself. If we observe conflict, the Qur'an demands repeated experimentation until the resolution of the conflict:

[He] who created seven heavens, tallied. You do not see in the creation of the Most Benignant any discrepancy; return your gaze, do you see any crevice? (Qur'an 67:3)[6].

Therefore, the Qur'an and science demand repeated experimentation and evidence to come to the truth.

The Qur'an is a book of guidance that asks its believers to investigate and understand nature. It does not spoon-feed them with knowledge, but advises them to observe and reflect on nature. An example of this method of teaching can be observed in the following verse:

And in the earth are signs [ayahs] for those who have firm faith, and in yourselves. (Qur'an: 51:20–21)[7]

The verses instruct that contemplating God's creation, pondering the open book of the universe, observing God's creative hand moving this universe, turning the pages of the book, and learning from human anatomy, all evoke true worship and remembrance of God. These and other verses encourage Muslims to examine the world with a scientist's eyes to understand the products and process of creation. Thus, our perception of the process of creation is enriched as we continue to study all pertinent verses of the Qur'an and to explore the universe as new technological means become available to us. To search for knowledge outside the Qur'an is a Muslim obligation. Imam Ghazzali (1058-1111) quotes from a sermon by Prophet Muhammad:

To be present in an assembly of learned men is better than praying one thousand *rek'at* (rounds) . . . Then the Prophet was asked: "O Messenger of God, is it better than the reading of the Qur'an?" He said:

"What benefit can the Qur'an do except through knowledge?" He said: "He who seeks knowledge to revive Islam and dies in that condition, there will be the difference of only one step between him and the prophets."[8]

The sermon made it very plain that all knowledge including from "the written scroll" that we call the universe, is necessary to understand Qur'anic knowledge. So, the search for the origin of the universe, life, and its means of operation must be taken as a core tenet of Islam.

The Qur'an and the Creation of the Universe

The Qur'an does not have a chapter on the genesis of our universe as do the Jewish and Christian scriptures. Many Christians and Jews believe that God created the universe in six days. Most contemporary Muslims also believe in the creation of the universe in "six days." The Qur'anic concept of the universe differs from that claimed by Herman Bondi, Thomas Gold, and Fred Hoyle, who claim that ours is a steady-state universe that never had a beginning and will continue to exist in a condition similar to its present. On the other hand, the universe, according to the Qur'an, has a beginning and an end, as we shall presently discuss. Knowledge of the external world is reflected in the sophistication of the language that people use. We invent new words to convey new knowledge. When the Qur'an came to Arabia, the people of that time and place used "the heavens and the earth" to describe the universe. The Qur'an describes the heavens and the earth (the universe) as a single entity that God split into the heavens (galaxies) and the earth.

Do not these unbelievers see that the heavens and the earth were an integrated mass, and then We split them and made every living thing from water? (Qur'an 21:30)[9]

The Qur'an further hints at our recent scientific discovery of the universe evolving from a gaseous state that is described as *smoke*.

And He turned to the heavens and it was a smoke. So He said to it and the earth: 'Come with willing obedience or perforce.' They said: 'We come willingly.' (Qur'an 41:11)[10]

According to modern cosmology, after its cosmic explosion, the universe began an expansion that has never ceased. The Qur'an also describes the universe as one that is expanding:

And it is We who have built the universe with [our creative] power; and it is We who are steadily expanding it." (Qur'an 51:47)[11]

In spite of this convergence of the scientific perception of the origin of the universe and the literal Qur'anic concept of Creation, many Muslims of our time are afraid that the big bang theory could be replaced by another paradigm and that if that happened, their faith might be weakened. A modern Islamic scholar, Muhammad Asad, argues:

It is, as a rule, futile to make an explanation of the Qur'an dependent on scientific findings, which may appear true today but may equally be disproved tomorrow by new findings.[12]

Whether or not the Qur'anic verses agree with modern science, these verses describe an explosive beginning of the universe from an integrated mass or singularity, its evolution through a gaseous state, and its continuing expansion.

A well-respected Muslim scholar, Al-Biruni (973–1048), agreed with the possibility of what I have described here in his book, *The Determination of the Coordinates of Positions for Correction of Distances between Cities*:

For it is quite possible that these [celestial] bodies were scattered . . . when the Creator designed and created them. If you then ask the mathematician as to the length of time, after which they would meet each other in a certain point, or before which they had met each other in that identical point, no blame attaches to him, if he speaks of billions of years.[13]

The Bible and the Qur'an agree that God created the Universe in six days. The six days of creation is not six earthly days, but eons. Al Biruni asks: "How is it possible to imagine that these days are like the days of our reckoning!" Then he rejects the reading of six days of creation as six solar days with a verse from Qur'an: "A day in the sight of thy Lord is like a thousand years of your reckoning." (Qur'an 22:47)[14]

The Future of the Universe

While the scientific data on the fate of the universe are derived from piecemeal experiments and observations by modern scientists, the Qur'anic description of the fate of the universe can be worked out from its account of the events that will take place before the day of resurrection. These descriptions of the events before the end of the universe are scattered over many chapters and verses in the Qur'an. The following verse indicates that the universe, including the earth, has an appointed term for existence:

We created not the heavens and the earth and all between them but for just ends, and for a term appointed . . ." (Qur'an 46:3)[15]

According to one view of science, in a few billions of years from now, the recession of the neighboring galactic systems will cease, and the process will start to reverse and end in the big crunch.

Based upon astronomical calculations, after the big bang the galaxies began to recede. Author and physicist Paul Davies states that according to the big bang–big crunch scenario, towards the end of the universe "the universe will not remain static, but will start contracting…Galaxies that are now receding from one another will start to approach instead."[16] The Qur'an also states that the receding galaxies would reverse their current courses. In the eighty-first Chapter of the Qur'an titled *Coiling Up* [of the universe], the receding galaxies would reverse their courses before the end of the universe: "So, I call to witness the stars that recede." (Qur'an 81:15)[17] Likewise, as the result of the final "rolling up" of the universe, astronomers would see the stars advancing (blue shift) toward them rather than receding (red shift), as they see today. The Qur'anic use of the phrase "receding stars" in the verse signals the expanding universe that was discussed earlier.

Before the final collapse even begins, astronomers believe that under the combined influence of hydrogen fusion on the solar surface and the high temperature helium fusion in its interior, the exterior of the sun will expand and cool.[18] This cooling of the sun may be what the Qur'an alludes to in a verse from the chapter, Coiling Up [of the universe]: "When the Sun shall be darkened." (Qur'an 81:1)[19] The sun will become a red giant star. When the sun enlarges it will swallow planets Mercury and Venus, and probably also Earth. The following verse seems to describe the "ruddy and bloated" sun: "Upon the day when heaven shall be as molten copper." (Qur'an 70:8)[20] The Qur'an speaks of a merger between the moon and the sun during the last days of the universe: "And the sun and moon are united."[21] (Qur'an 75:9) It does not mention other planets of the solar system because the common Arabic language at the time of revelation did not include the words Mercury and Venus. However, all Arabs definitely knew of the moon. The sun gradually becomes red and its overwhelming heat melts Arctic and Antarctic ice, resulting in coastal flooding throughout the world. Similarly, the Qur'an states that the last days of the universe will be heralded by rising water levels in the oceans and by flooding along the coasts: "[On the Last Day] And the ocean filled with swell." (Qur'an 52:6)[22] The Arabic verb *sajara* in the text of this verse means, "to fill." According to current cosmology, flooding of the continental coasts is the result of the "filling" of the ocean due to the melting ice of the poles. Science points out that as the collapse continues, the soaring ocean temperature will lift clouds of steam into the air. Finally, the unforgiving extreme heat from the sun will make the oceans boil. In the chapter, *Coiling Up*, the Qur'an seems to be ahead of its time in warning us about the last days of the universe "When the sea shall be set boiling." (Qur'an 81:6)[23]

According to Paul Davies, well-known author and physicist, during the collapse of the universe "observers would no longer be able to discern individual galaxies for these would now have begun to merge with each other as intergalactic space closes up."[24] What Paul Davies states is similar to the Qur'anic revelation that the observable shining points in the sky will decrease during the merger of the galaxies such that the sky appears empty: [On the Last Day] "when the sky stripped bare." (Qur'an 81:11)[25]

According to the big bang–big crunch scenario, as the end of the current universe approaches, initially the galaxies, and then the stars will collapse and merge into each other until it becomes a cataclysmic inferno. The continuing collapse of the universe will result in a singularity identical to where our universe originally began. The Qur'an, in the following verses, seems to narrate the events of the last days of the universe, like a modern astronomer describing the events of the vanishing universe: "The day the heaven shall be rent asunder with the clouds." (Qur'an 25:25)[26] The "clouds" may be those originating from the boiling ocean. "And [on the day] the earth is moved, and its mountains and they are crushed to powder at one stroke." (Qur'an 69:14)[27] "When the sky cleft asunder, when the stars are scattered." (Qur'an 82: 1–2)[28] "When the stars fall, losing their luster." (Qur'an 81: 2)[29] "When the sky is rent asunder and it becomes red like ointment." (Qur'an 55:37)[30] "It will be no more than a single blast." (Qur'an 36:53)[31] The events that the Qur'an describes seem to fit the formation of black dwarfs supernovae, and the final event of the universe collapsing into singularity.

What happens after the big crunch? When the collapse of the universe is complete, all the matter in the universe will be compressed into a single point. At this point of infinite space-time curvature, every atom and every particle in our universe will be crushed out of existence. This point becomes a state of singularity—a single point of space and time, where density and temperature become infinite and theories of science become invalid. One might speculate that there would be new laws that worked in singularities, but, according to Stephen Hawking, it would be highly problematic even to formulate such laws at such unruly points, and our observations would not help us to define what those laws might be. Whether the universe will rise again phoenix-like from the singularity is not known. Should the universe rise again, Carl Sagan asked, what would be the nature and properties of the new universe?[32] Would the laws of physics and chemistry that would govern the new universe be different? In the universe that springs out of the big crunch, would there be stars and galaxies, or something quite different?

The following Qur'anic verse seems to introduce, in the layman's language of the Arab, our current scientific prediction of the coming big crunch, and answers the above questions:

The day when We shall roll up the heaven as a scroll is rolled for writings; as We originated first creation, so *We shall bring it back again* — a promise binding on Us; So We shall do. (Qur'an 21:104)[33]

The literal meaning of this verse above suggests a new universe will spring out of the singularity. Similarly, the following Qur'anic verse could be the answer to Carl Sagan's questions.

On the day when earth is changed into different earth and heavens into new heavens, Mankind shall stand before God, the One, who conquers all. (Qur'an 14:48)[34]

The verse suggests that, after the big crunch, the newly created universe will be based on new laws of physics and chemistry and may be based on different mathematics. Two plus two may not become four.

The new universe of the Hereafter would not have our current time-space relationship as suggested by the following verses:

The day [The Day of judgment] these people see seems to them as though they had stayed [in the world or in the state of death] only for an afternoon of a day or its forenoon. (Qur'an 79:46)[35]

On the Day when He shall gather them [unto Himself, it will seem to them] as if they had not tarried [on earth] longer than an hour of a day, knowing one another; [and] lost indeed will be they who [in their lifetime] considered it a lie that they were destined to meet God, and [thus] failed to find the right way. (Qur'an 10:45)[36]

In summary, we find much agreement between Qur'anic revelation and scientific discoveries about the origin and some of the theories about the fate of our current universe. Both maintain that the universe originated from nothing and evolved into its present state over a long period of earthbound time. They agree that the universe is expanding and that at some remote future, it will collapse into a single entity or singularity where existing physical and chemical laws become nonexistent, mathematics would not add up, and numbers become infinite. Not only the Qur'an but also some scientists believe in the rise of a new universe.

The big bang–big crunch scenario has been seriously questioned lately by astronomers who have observed an acceleration of the expansion of the universe. They claim that as the universe expands, it will freeze into the heat death. The amount of matter and energy contained in the universe determines whether the universe is going to freeze to death or collapse to become the big crunch. Dark energy currently accounts for almost three-quarters of the total mass-energy of the universe. Similarly, dark matter accounts for the vast majority of mass in the observable universe. It cannot be observed and cannot be weighed. We know almost nothing of the physics of dark energy and the chemistry of dark matter. Therefore, the final scientific verdict on the theories of the heat death or the big crunch is yet to be made. Moreover, the observation of the increased acceleration of the expansion of the universe does not preclude some other as yet unknown attracting forces coming to bear on the accelerating universe, reversing the expansion, and ending in the big crunch.

Al-Baari, the Fountainhead of Evolution.

Next we will explore the creation/evolution of life in terms of the Islamic context. Many Christians and Jews believe that God created human beings in His image and created Eve from Adam's rib. Most contemporary Muslims also believe in the story of the creation of Eve from Adam's rib. Their understanding is based upon oral traditions collected and attributed to the Prophet Muhammad (570-632) over 200 years after his demise by Muhammad ibn Ismail al-Bukhari (810-870). However, not a single verse in the Qur'an supports this belief. Then what is the Qur'anic narrative on the topic of human origin? Verses about the origin of life and humans are scattered throughout the Qur'an. We have collected the key verses in order to develop a clear picture of the meanings they convey.

A casual reading of the verses may give us the impression that they contradict each other, but apparent contradictions evaporate when we interpret the meanings of all the verses collectively rather than the meaning of each single verse. More importantly, our conclusions should be consistent with our overall reading of the Qur'an. Muslims accept the Qur'anic claim that its internal consistency is proof of its divine origin:

Do they not consider the Qur'an [with care]? Had it been from other than God, they would have found therein much discrepancy. (Qur'an 4:82)[37]

The Qur'an informs us that God created the universe and its components, including its laws and forces, in accordance with His grand design, that God is manifested through His creations, and that His attributes are the link between human beings and their comprehension of the Divine. Out of the ninety-nine attributes ascribed to God in the Qur'an, four grant us insight into His process of creation. Those key attributes are *Rabb* (the Sustainer), al-*Khaliq* (the Creator), al-*Baari* (the Evolver), and al-*Musawwir* (the Bestower of Forms).

The first command that came to the Prophet appears in the first and second verses that were revealed to him: "Read in the name of thy Sustainer (*Rabb*), who has created; created man out of a germ-cell."[39] (Qur'an 96:1–2) The general translation of the word Rabb as Sustainer does not convey its overall meaning. The noun Rabb is derived from the Arabic word *Rububiyat*, the meaning of which cannot be fully rendered in English with one word. Based on his analysis of the works of early Arab lexicographers, Abul Kalam Azad, a Muslim Qur'anic scholar and commentator from the Indian subcontinent, deciphers the meaning of the word as follows:

To develop a thing, stage by stage, in accordance with its inherent aptitude and needs, its different aspects of existence and also in the manner affording the requisite freedom for it to attain its full stature.[39]

Likewise, Imam Abdul-Qasim ar-Raghib (eleventh century), in his book *Al-Mufradat fi Gharib al-Qur'an* (*The Vocabulary of The Qur'an*), defines the meaning of the word Rabb as follows:

Rabb signifies the fostering of a thing in such a manner as to make it attain one condition after another until it reaches its goal of perfection.[40]

The major components of the meaning of the word Rububiyat are thus: (a) development of a thing by an external agent; (b) a step-by-step process, not an instant event; and (c) the freedom for the objects "to attain full stature" within the overall creative process. Therefore, Rabb, the derived noun from Rububiyat, means an evolver. The use of the noun Rabb as an attribute of God suggests that God lets organisms evolve, affording them the freedom to attain complete perfection within the limits of His laws of nature.

Another name of God is al-*Khaliq* (The Creator). The word is derived from the Arabic root verb *khalaqa*, which is used in nearly all the verses pertaining to the creation of human beings and the universe as a whole. Almost all commentators and translators of the Qur'an, both Muslim and non-Muslim, translate the meaning of this verb as corresponding to the English verb "to create." However, this translation does not convey the original and complete meaning of the verb. Edward William Lane's (1801–1876) *The Arabic-English Lexicon* guides non-Arabic speaking students of the Qur'an to understand its meaning. According to Lane, the verb *khalaqa* means "proportioning a thing into another thing" and "to bring a thing into existence according to a certain measure, or proportion, and so as to make it equal to (another thing)." It also signifies "the originating, or to bring a thing into existence after it had not been, or the bringing a thing into existence from a state of non-existence."[41] Hence, there are three components to the meaning of the word *khalaqa*: (a) shaping an original substance or entity into another object ("proportioning a thing to another thing"); (b) identifying the newly formed object or creature separately from its original source by its own peculiar characteristics—not like father and son, but like a tree to a canoe or single original cell to a human and other life forms; and (c) bringing into being the newly formed object or creature with its characteristic features, which were nonexistent before its original birth ("to bring a thing into existence from a state of non-existence"). In this process the new creature becomes a prototype. Therefore, the classical meaning of the Arabic word *khalaqa* can be summarized as follows: To bring a thing into existence according to a certain measure, or proportion, so as to make it equal to another thing that is not pre-existing. Therefore, *al-Khaliq*, one of the descriptive titles of God, means that God makes things to evolve.

The Qur'an describes God as "the Evolver" (*al-Baari*) and "the Bestower of forms" (*al-Musawwir*), reinforcing the idea of creation as a stage-by-stage process. The verse reads: "He is God, the Creator (*al-Khaliq*), the Evolver (*al-Baari*) and the Bestower of forms (*al-Musawwir*)." (Qur'an 59:24)[42] *Al-Baari*, the Arabic word in the above verse, is derived from the verb *baara*, which means "a thing is becoming clear from another thing either by being released therefrom" or by "evolution from a previously created matter or state."[43] So God, the executor of such evolution, is *al-Baari* (the Evolver). The word *al-Musawwir* is derived from the verb *sawwara*, which means to sculpt a thing and give definite form or color to make things exactly suitable for a certain end or object. Hence God is called *al-Musawwir*, or the "sculptor, of all existing things, who has established them, given to every one of them a special form and a particular manner of being whereby it is distinguished, with their variety and multitude."[44] Therefore, the meanings of *Rabb*, *al-Khaliq*, *al-Baari*, and *al-Musawwir* indicate that evolution and creation are not contradictory but mutually complementary. In this context, while creation is a divine process, the theory of evolution is a summary of the human observation of that divine process.

Creation: A Gradual Process

The Qur'an reads: "I created you before you were nothing." (Qur'an 19:9)[45] Therefore, mankind and the universe were created from nonexistence when there was no time or space. When the Qur'an refers to a state of nothingness, it does not mean that human beings were created instantaneously without any connection to other life forms or species. The Qur'an says that the creation of the universe and its contents was not an instant event, but a process: "It is He who beginneth the process of creation (khalaq) and repeats it." (Qur'an 10-4.)[46] Yusuf Ali, a well-known Muslim translator, explains: God's creation is not a simple act, once done and finished with. It is continuous, and there are many stages, not the least important of which is the Hereafter, when the fruits of our life will be achieved.[47]

Yusuf Ali's commentary is further enhanced by the following verse, "Who created (khalaqa) you, then proportioned you into whatever form He willed. He made you out of components (rakkaba)." (Qur'an 82:7–8) The verb rakkaba in the original Arabic text of this verse means "to create a thing from components; put or set one part of it upon another."[48] Therefore, the verse indicates that the necessary components were created as prerequisites for the creation of man.

The phrase, "He began", in verse 32:7, ("He began the creation of man with [nothing more than] clay")[49] indicates that the beginning was not an end in itself. Additional steps necessarily followed to complete the intended task. Other verses also clearly imply a time lapse, for example: "He fashioned (khalaqa) you from sounding clay, like unto pottery." (Qur'an 55:14)[50] The word fakha'ar, in the Arabic text of the Qur'an, means "baked pottery or a baked vessel of clay."[51] We can read this verse as follows: "Just as clay is molded into shape in stages and baked into pottery, the prototype human was also created through successive stages over a period of earthly time." This inference is supplemented in the following verses: "He fashioned you, and perfected your shapes," (Qur'an 64:3)[52] and "He created (khalaqa) you in successive stages." (Qur'an 71:14)[53] The latter verse unequivocally states that the creation of the human species was not a magical ex nihilo instant event of earthly time, but a step-by-step transformation. Likewise, the late Stephen Jay Gould, famous paleontologist, describes the "creation by stages" as follows:

Evolution usually proceeds by 'speciation'—the splitting of one lineage from a parental stock—not by the slow and steady transformation of these large parental stocks. Repeated episodes of speciation produce a bush."[54]

Even though the Qur'an states that God created humans in successive stages, it does not describe all the stages of their evolution from clay before they became Homo sapiens sapiens (modern man). Sperm and ova are not human. The forty-six chromosomes present in the fertilized human egg are the encapsulated codes of a future human being, but we do not use the term man or woman to describe them. They are still a bundle of amino acids, phosphate and sugar. A thing is named only when it comes into its own form and acquires specific characteristics. For example, a few of the stages through which human beings came into existence have their own names—water, clay, soil, microorganism, marine animals, mammal-like reptiles, insect eating primate, Dryopithecus, Australopithecus, *Homo erectus* and Cro-Magnon man. However, all of those are only landmarks in the journey of the creation of the modern human species (*Homo sapiens sapiens*). These stages took place a long time ago, and memories of this do not remain in the human brain, but are stored in the vestigial structures, fossils, chemistry, immunology, and so on. Those unremembered stages of evolution in the creation of the modern human species might be what the following verse alludes to: "Has there come on man a while of time when he was a thing unremembered?" (Qur'an 76:1)[55] The verse suggests that the human species existed in some kind of form that was not recognizable as human. Perhaps this was one among many verses that may have inspired Jalaluddin Rumi (1207-1273), a famous Muslim sage, to compose the following strophe in his *Masnavi*, 600 years before Charles Darwin:

He came first to the inorganic realm and from there stepped over to the vegetable kingdom. Living long as a plant he had no memory of his struggles in the inorganic realm. Similarly rising from the plant to the animal life he forgets his plant life retaining only an attraction for it which he feels especially in the spring, ignorant of the secret and cause of this attraction like the infant at the breast who knows not why he is attracted to the mother. Then the creator draws him from animality towards humanity. So, he went from realm to realm until he became rational.[56]

A sampling of some Qur'anic verses confirms the idea that humans are linked to both organic and inorganic realms: "We fashioned man from quintessence of clay." (Qur'an 23:12)[57] One may conclude that man was created from an extract of clay. Or is there another meaning to the verse? Montmorillonite clay has been shown to have the property to form phosphodiester bonds. A phosphodiester bond is a bond between two sugar groups and a phosphate group. A diester bond links two nucleotides together to form DNA and RNA, the nucleotide polymers. These bonds are central to all life on Earth, as they make up the backbone of the strands of DNA. Initial studies established that some montmorillonite clays catalyze condensation of activated mononucleotides to oligomers.[58] Does "fashioned from quintessence of clay" in the above Qur'anic verse mean montmorillonite clay was a catalyst in the phosphodiester bonding in the pre-biotic soup?

Human: A Genus of Animal

Almost all biologists accept the fact that life originated in water and so does the Qur'an: "We made every living thing from the water?" (Qur'an 21:30)[59] "Every living thing (*minal-maa-'i kulla shay-'in hayy*)" in the verse certainly includes mankind. Therefore, the early stage of the evolution of the human species occurred in water. Yet another verse states: "And God has created (*khalaqa*) every living animal from water: Of them some that creep on their bellies: Some walk on two legs: Some walk on four: God created what He wills: For verily God has power over all things ... (*Wallaahu khalaqa kulla daaabbatinmim-maaa': fa-minhum-mny-yamshii 'alaa batnih; wa minhum-mǎny-yamshii 'alaa rijlayn; wa min-hum-mǎny-yamshii 'alaaa 'Araba'*)." (Qur'an 24:45).[60]

Verse 21:30 uses the phrase "We made from water every living thing (*minal-maa-'i kulla shay-'in hay*)." Verse 24:45 offers additional clarification with use of the phrase, "every animal (*kulla daaabatim-mim-maaa*)." This verse specifies that animals were created from water and explains the categories included among animals by their method of movement. Humans and sometimes apes are the only living creatures that always walk on two legs, while birds can fly and walk on two legs. Therefore, the two legged animals mentioned in verse 24:45 could be either bird or ape or human being.

The grammatical structure of the above verse with the phrase *fa min hum* is highly significant. If the noun *dabbah* (animals) were applied only to rational or irrational creatures separately, the two phrases, *fa min-hunna* or *fa-min-ha,* would have been used in proper Arabic grammar. Instead, the Qur'anic use of thephrase *fa min hum* in the verse reveals that the Arabic noun *dabbah* (animals) in the verse refers to both rational and irrational creatures. Therefore, the verse states that a rational animal that walks on two legs was also created from water.[61] Humans are the only creatures who walk on two legs all the time. Humans are the most rational of all creatures. Therefore, the rational animal that walks on two legs referred to in the verse is human and so, humans belong to the animal kingdom. Therefore, more than 400 hundred years before the publication of *The Origin of Species* (1859), the Muslim scholar, Ibn-Khaldun wrote in *Muqaddimah* (1377), "[M]an belongs to the genus of animals and God distinguished him from them by the ability to think, which He gave man and through which man is able to arrange his actions in an orderly manner."[62]

Creation of *Homo Sapiens Sapiens*

`We learned from the Qur'an that the creation process is evolutionary.

Moreover, many medieval pre–Charles Darwin Muslim scholars held the view that humankind evolved from the animal world. However, most *contemporary* Muslims believe that Adam was created *ex nihilo* and that Eve was created from his rib. Here we will explore the Qur'an to choose between the two beliefs. First, consider the following two verses:

O you man, what deluded you concerning your Munificent Lord, who created you (*khalaqa*), fashioned you (*sawwa*) and shaped you in perfection (*hadala*). (Qur'an 82:6–7)[63]

And We who created (*khalaqa*) you, and fashioned (*sawwara*) you, then told the Angels: fall ye prostrate before Adam! And they fell prostrate, all save Satan, who was not of those who make prostration. (Qur'an 7:11)[64]

If God created Adam with no connection to the animal world and other hominids, the Qur'an would not have said, "We created you, then fashioned you." Similarly, if Adam did not evolve in stages but was a perfect creation, then the verb to sculpt (*sawwa* or *sawwara*), which appears in the verses, becomes superfluous because there is nothing to perfect in a perfect being. The modern commentator translates the verb *hadala* as "shaped you in perfection." Lane's *Arabic-English Lexicon* gives another meaning to this word: "rate a thing as equal to a thing of another kind so as to make it like the latter." Therefore, the word means to transform a thing into another, so that the latter is distinctly identifiable from the former. In support of this meaning, Lane quotes the following Qur'anic verse: "All praise be to God who created the heavens and the earth, and ordained darkness and light. Yet the unbelievers make others equal (*hadala*) of their Lord." (Qur'an 6:1)

Lane gives the phrase (*phulaanan biphulaanin hadala*), which means, "He made such a one to be equal, or like, such a one."[65] Therefore, when we translate verses 82:6–7, they must be rephrased as: O you man, what deluded you concerning your Munificent Lord, who shaped you from a preexisting thing (*khalaqa*), sculpted you (*sawwa*), and transformed you (*hadala*) to [distinctly identifiable] perfect human shape (i.e., *Homo sapiens sapiens*).

Similarly if we replace the words "created and fashioned" with the meaning of *khalaqa* and *sawwara* of the classical Arabic, the translation of verse 7:11 would read: And We who shaped you from a pre-existing thing (*khalaqa*), and sculpted or perfected you to become distinguished with modern human (*Homo sapiens sapiens*) characteristics (*sawwarra*), then told the Angels: fall ye prostrate before Adam! And they fell prostrate, all save Satan, who was not of those who make prostration.

We have learned earlier the divine epithet *al-Musawwir* (sculptor) could also mean, in current scientific vernacular, someone who creates a distinct species. Therefore, *al-Musawwir* created perfect human beings sculpted from a previously created hominid species. Verse 6:133 gives explicit evidence that modern humans were evolved from earlier hominids. "Thy Lord is All-sufficient, Merciful. If He will, He can put you away, and leave after you, to succeed you, what He will, as He produced you from the seed of another people." (Qur'an 6:133)[66] The context in verse 130 of the same chapter shows that it is addressed to mankind. Almost all translators of the Qur'an render the Arabic word *ansha* as "raised." This is not a correct translation of the word, however. Lane translates it as follows: "originated it; brought it into being or existence; made it, or produced it for the first time, it not having been before."[67]

Initially, verse 6:133 states that God may replace modern humans with another species ("whomever He pleases to succeed you"). The process of the creation of the new species (*khalifah*) from human seed is similar to when God "produced humanity into existence for the first time." The verse also suggests that the human species was originally created from "the seeds of another people," i.e., that modern humans were evolved from earlier people. Therefore, verse 6:133 can be rephrased as: Thy Lord is all Self-sufficient, Merciful. If He will, He can put you away, and leave after you, to succeed you, what He will, as He originally created you [as a species] from the seed of another people.

A respected twelfth-century exegete of the Qur'an, Fakhr al-Din al-Razi (1149–1209), explains the verse similarly: [God] said: 'As We created you from the seeds of a different people.' For a wise person, were he to contemplate on this statement . . . he would know that the Almighty created mankind from a sperm; a sperm that did not contain his picture (genotype) in any form or way.[68]

I translated the word, *khalifah*, in the above verse 6:133 as "species." However, most Muslim commentators of the Qur'an translate the noun *khalifah*, in the above verse, as "vicegerent." Human as vicegerent means that the human species as a whole is the deputy appointed to act on the authority of God, especially in administrative duties. This word, *khalifah*, is actually derived from the verb *khalafah*, which means "one entity that succeeds another or remains after another that has perished or died."[69]

Therefore, the literal translation of the noun *khalifah* is "successor," but the term vicegerent is also correct, because human supremacy over the earth was established by divine revelation of all knowledge to human beings through the Prophet Adam. According to biology, *Homo sapiens sapiens* as a species "succeeded or remained after" the earlier hominid inhabitants of the earth "that had perished or died." Therefore, logically a new species is a *khalifah*. We have paleontological data that pre-modern human species existed and perished with the emergence of modern humankind. This early hominid was identified by Ibn-Arabi (1165-1240) and other early Muslims as an animal-like man, but modern biologists called him *Homo erectus*, Cro-Magnon, or other such names.

Population Bottleneck: The Question of Adam and Eve

Most Muslims, if asked about Adam and Eve, will state that they were the very first of humankind on the face of the earth and that every human being of the past and current age is a genetic descendant of this primordial couple. But this belief crumbles under scientific scrutiny. "Population bottleneck" is the scientific term for a natural event in which a significant percentage of a population or species is killed or otherwise prevented from reproducing, and the population is reduced. Eventually, this continuing deterioration of species vigor leads to its extinction. Small and isolated species populations are known to suffer dire consequences when there is a lack of genetic diversity.

Detrimental genetic diseases are very common in small, interbred populations, and genetic vulnerability coupled with a lack of genetic diversity can lead to the extinction of such a population. The smaller the population, the greater the probability it would disappear. The smallest possible population of human species is two people, where naturally genetic variation is extremely limited. Therefore, the consideration that the proliferation of the human species could have resulted from only two ancestors, such as Adam and Eve, is not plausible by scientific criteria. The human species would have become extinct due to the extreme population bottleneck.

In order to determine the role played by Adam and Eve in the history of the human species, we need to have an understanding of human soul-body relationship based on the Qur'an.

The Creation of Human Souls

Many Muslims use the Qur'anic verse 4:1 to discredit the theory of evolution. With the definition of humans as above, these verses definitely do not conflict with the theory.

O mankind, venerate your Lord, who created you from a single soul, from it created its mate, and from the pair of them has spread abroad countless men and women. (Qur'an 4:1)[70]

The creation of the human from a "single soul" and "from it . . .its mate (duality)" refers to the creation of the primordial human soul and its progression into a dyad in the generation of the male and female human souls, not yet clothed in the garment of biological flesh. Out of these two souls, God created all other human souls. What the verse refers to here is not the creation of visible metaphorical humans in flesh and blood, but the creation of real humans manifested as spirits.

The Dual Nature of the Human Species

A complex metaphor can be confused easily with reality. When we use pronouns such as "I" or "you," we recognize the person based upon the physical features of his or her material body. By doing so, we in fact deny our own spiritual existence from a medical and Qur'anic point of view.

Surgeons transplant hearts, lungs, pancreas, kidneys, hands, even faces onto the soul's outer garment of flesh and blood. Soon surgeons will be transplanting laboratory-grown body parts into *Homo sapiens sapiens*. Still each human soul maintains its individuality and acts in the material world as he/she did before surgery if there is no damage to the brain. Therefore, if a physical body is taken out of the comprehensive human context, it is only a machine with component parts that can be modified or, if possible, replaced.

The dual nature of the human body and soul is made very clear in the Qur'an as well as by a saying of Prophet Muhammad. According to the Qur'an, the soul is created and everlasting. It is alive and movable. So, "God gathers up the souls of those who do not die, in their sleep; then He keeps back those ordained for death, and sends the others back for an appointed term." (Qur'an 39:42)[71] Hence, the material body can remain alive even when the soul is temporarily taken out from the sleeping body, showing the dual nature. Moreover, according to sayings of the Prophet, a fetus is alive, but without soul until the 120th day of intrauterine life when the soul is breathed into a fetus by an angel.[72]

Verses 36:65 and 41:20–21 state that material body parts will testify against souls on the Day of Judgment: "This day [Judgment Day] We seal their mouths, and their hands speak to Us and their feet will bear witness concerning what they earned." Qur'an 36:65)[73] "Their ears and their eyes and their skins will testify against them as to what they used to do. And they say unto their skins: 'Why did you testify against us?' They say: 'God, who gave all things power of articulation, made us to speak.' " (Qur'an 41:20–21)[74]

While the human spirit is accountable on the Day of Judgment, its outer garment, made out of flesh and blood, is not. Therefore, the human spirit is separate from the physical body, which is only a visible metaphor and a product of evolution on the earth. Similarly, the material body is only the robotic arm of the soul. However, on the Day of Judgment, humans will be raised up with all parts of their body as they were on the earth. The chapter, "The Resurrection," states: "Does man think We shall not put his bones together? Surely We are able to re-form even his fingertips."

The infusion of the human soul is necessary for *Homo sapiens sapiens* to become a perfect human in the Islamic context. God elevated *Homo sapiens sapiens* above non-physical beings, angels and *jinns*, only after the infusion of a human soul into it. God asked angels and *jinns* "And when I have fashioned him and after breathed into him my spirit, bow before him in homage." (Qur'an 15:29)[76]

Adam: The Spiritual, not Biological, Parent

Next we will discuss the creation of the Prophet Adam. There are four steps in the creation of Adam: the creation of the soul of Adam; the creation of Adam's outer garment, the physical body; the infusion of Adam's soul; and the elevation of Adam to become the first prophet by revealing the divine message to him. These steps are described in verse 15:29 (quoted above) and verse 2:31 ("Then He gave Adam knowledge of the nature and reality of all things and everything."[77]), which describe the creation of Adam's physical body and the infusion of his soul into his body. Ordinary humans become prophets only when God reveals His wisdom to them. So, God elevated Adam to become the first of His long chain of prophets by teaching him "knowledge of the nature and reality of all things and everything." (Qur'an 2:31) Then God blessed them to live in a spiritual "Garden" of ease, happiness, and innocence.

Muslims believe that Islam is the religion of all of the prophets. This belief is based upon the following verses:

The Religion before God is Islam. (Qur'an 3:19)[78]

Say: We believe in God, and what has been sent down to us, and what has been revealed to Abraham, Ismael, Isaac, Jacob, and their progeny, and that which was given to Moses and Christ, and to all other prophets by the Lord: We make no distinction among them, we submit to Him (Qur'an 2:136)[79]

No; Abraham in truth was not a Jew, neither a Christian but he was a Muslim. (Qur'an 3:67)[80]

According to these verses, all prophets preached Islam and so they are all Muslims. Adam being the first prophet of God preaching Islam, he and his mate became the original spiritual parents of all humans.

If Adam was the first prophet, he must have had a human community to whom to preach the divine message. Let us explore whether there is any evidence for the existence of a community of human species as contemporaries of Adam.

Evidence for Human Contemporaries of the Prophet Adam

The Qur'an (82:6-7) states: the Munificent Lord "shaped you [human] from a pre-existing thing (*khalaqa*), sculpted you (*sawwa*), and transformed you to [distinctly identifiable] perfect human shape (*hadala*)." The verses describe a God-directed evolutionary process that led to the creation of the visible outer DNA based garments of real humans, which modern biologists named *Homo sapiens sapiens*. Then verses 7:10–11 describe the creation and the settlement of the initial human community on the earth before the creation of the Prophet Adam. The verses state: "Certainly We have established you [humankind] in the earth and made in it means of livelihood for you; little it is that you give thanks. We who created you, and fashioned you, then told the Angels: fall ye prostrate before Adam! And they fell prostrate, all save Iblis (Satan), who was not of those who make prostration." (Qur'an 7:10–11)[81]

A close examination of the grammatical structure of the verses is very important. In many languages, verbs are conjugated in relation to the number of individuals to which the action applies. In English, every noun is either singular or plural. Every verb is modified to comply with a singular or plural noun or pronoun. Unlike English, Arabic has singular, dual and plural forms of pronouns, nouns, verbs, and adjectives. The singular form is used when referring to one person or thing, the dual refers to two people or two things and the plural form for more than two people or things.

> Certainly
> We have established you [humankind] (plural)
> in the earth
> and made for you (plural)
> in it
> livelihood
> And certainly
> Who Created you (plural)
> Fashioned you (plural)
> then
> told the Angels: fall ye prostrate before Adam!

The grammatical construction of the verses with the plural in (established you), (made in it), (created you), and (fashioned you) is the confirmation that the initial part of the verse does not speak of the creation and the settlement of Adam on the earth, but of the creation and settlement of the initial human community. God blessed the original community of human species with the Prophet Adam as their guide and only "then " God asked angels and *jinn* to prostrate themselves before Adam. There are additional Qur'anic reasons to believe in the existence of human contemporaries with Adam.

The following Qur'anic verses 2:35–36[82] narrate the account of the expulsion of Adam and Eve from the "Garden."

> And We said:
> O! Adam (singular)

You dwell (singular)
You (singular)
and your mate (singular)
in the garden
and you two eat (dual)
from it
eat freely as
you two wish (dual)
and you two approach not (dual)
this tree
lest you two become (dual)
transgressors.
Then Satan made them to slip (dual)
from it
and send the two out (dual)
from that (State) the two (dual)
were in. (dual)
And We (God) said:
'Get you down.' (plural)
Some of you (plural)
are enemies to others; (plural)
and you have (plural)
in the earth a habitation
and sustenance for a while.

Verse 2:35 begins with a singular noun and pronoun, indicating Adam; then changes to a dual pronoun, referring to both Adam and Eve. The Arabic verb used in the Divine command to get out of the "Garden" in verse 36 after the violation of the Divine guidance, is conjugated, however, not with the dual form, but with the extended plural indicating more than two subjects. Medieval Muslim scholars have interpreted this in two different ways. The command in plural, "get you down," is directed to a group consisting of Adam, Eve and Satan. The second proposes that the command is given to a group consisting of Adam, Eve and their future, yet-to-be-born descendants. Both of these interpretations invariably lead us to a genetically unviable bottleneck that would have predisposed early humanity to extinction.

As the interpretations of the early Muslim scholars do not find credence within a realistic biological model, I offer a third interpretation. This interpretation is compatible with scientific understandings. Returning to verses 2:35–36, initially Adam and Eve are addressed while in the Garden as "you" in the dual grammatical form when God offered them to enjoy the "Garden." Adam was nevertheless deemed a Prophet.

Adam must have had contemporary human beings by whom he was ordained to convey the Divine message. God ordered them to "get you down" from their paradisiacal mental state of perfect ease and happiness when the Prophet Adam and his congregation, the trustees of God on the earth, violated the divine guidance. The use of the plural form, ("get you down"), in the divine command suggests the presence of a generation of human beings along with Adam and Eve. Then, the Qur'an states, "Some of you are enemies to others." The use of the plural form, (some of you), referring to a group of human beings is another reason to suppose that there were other human beings with Adam and Eve. So, based on Qur'anic verses 2:35–36 and 7:10–11, God peopled the world of Adam and Eve with rich genetic diversity so that His vicegerents would not go extinct due to population bottleneck until the end of the world.

The Theory of Evolution and Pre-Darwin Muslims

So far the discussion had been to establish the fact that there is no conflict between the theory of evolution and the Qur'anic script of the human story on Earth. I began my journey searching for the religious answer to the question of human origins after my son, Zaifi, then a high school student, asked me, "Dad, you send me to the best school around our home to study science. You send me to the Islamic Center to study the Qur'an. Science says that human beings evolved from the world of apes, but the Islamic Center teaches us that humans were initially created in heaven and came to Earth fully formed. What is the truth?" A few months later, I told my son a shortened Qur'anic story of the origin of the human species that I described here. Then, he asked, "Dad! Did Muslims before Darwin believe in the evolution of life and man?" Later, I learned that many early Muslim scholars such as Al-Jahiz (776–868), Ibn-Miskawaayah (930–1030), Al-Biruni (930–1030), and others living close to the birth of Islam believed in the evolutionary origin of life, plants, and animals, including humans. For example, Abu Bakr Muhammed ibn-Arabi (1165-1240), one of the foremost interpreters of the Qur'an, explains in his book, *Uqlatu'l-Mustawfiz* (*Controller of the Wanderer*) the concept of the "perfect man" as being God's intended vicegerent on Earth. In order for a human being to become God's deputy on Earth, he had to evolve into a perfect form. Ibn-Arabi makes a distinction between a "perfect man" and an inferior form, which he calls "animal man." The latter is "not a man" because he exhibits qualities peculiar to animals. His relationship to a human being is like "that of the ape to the animal man." In Ibn-Arabi's view, if man does not reach the stage of perfection, he is an animal whose appearance resembles the external appearance of man. Thus, it was God's intention for human beings to evolve into their perfect form[s] so they would be suitable vicegerents of the Universe.[83]

Similarly, Islam's greatest historiographer, Abd-ar-Rahman Muhammed ibn-Khaldun (1332-1406), believed that the creation of mankind was gradual and that humans evolved from the world of apes. He writes in *Muqaddimah* (*An Introduction to History*) a few centuries before Charles Darwin:

"One should then look at the world of creation. It started out from the minerals and progressed, in an ingenious, gradual manner to plants and animals. The last stage of minerals is connected with the first stage of plants, such as herbs, and seedless plants. The last stage of plants such as palms and vines is connected with the first stage of animals, such as snails and shellfish, which have only the power to touch. The word 'connection' with regard to these created things means that the last stage of each group is fully prepared to become the first stage of the next group. The animal world then widens, its species become numerous, and, in a gradual process of creation, it finally leads to man, who is able to think and reflect. The higher stage of man is reached from the world of monkeys, in which both sagacity and perception are found, but which has not reached the stage of actual reflection and thinking. At this point we come to the first stage of man [after the world of monkeys]. This is as far as our [physical] observation extends."[84]

According to Ibn-Khaldun, species are not fixed, but subject to changes with a changing environment. He teaches that the physical characteristics of organisms are determined by their "essence." So, he explains the transformation of life by Nature as follows: The essences at the end of each particular stage of the worlds are by nature prepared to be transformed into the essences adjacent to them, either above or below.

He maintained that active nature (*kiyan*) "has the ability to generate substances and change essences."[85]

If we replace the phrase, "generate substances and change essences" with our modern scientific terms, mutation and genotype, we get a clear picture of Ibn-Khaldun's understanding of the origin of species. The quote from Ibn-Khadun reads as follows: active nature (*kiyan*) "has the ability to generate mutations (substances) and change genotypes (essences)."

Not even the human species is isolated and protected from the ever-changing influence of the active nature. Ibn-Khaldun, after describing the influence of environmental factors in the origin of human races, concludes his view as follows: Physical circumstances and the environment are subject to changes that affect later generations; they do not necessarily remain unchanged.[86]

According to him, earthly existence is a continuum of transformations of essences that occur in stages in a natural order of ascent and descent. He describes the transformation of species into other species as a result of the modification of essence (genotype) by nature:

The essences at the end of each particular stage of the worlds (i.e., different species) are by nature prepared to be transformed into the essence adjacent to them. This is the case with the simple material elements; it is the case with the palms and vines [which constitute] the last stage of plants, in their relation to snails and shellfish, [which constitute] the [lowest] stage of animals. It is also the case with monkeys, creatures combining in themselves cleverness and perception, in their relation to man, the being who has the ability to think and to reflect.

The preparedness [for transformation] that exists on either side, at each stage of the worlds, is meant when [we speak about] their connection.[87]

If he were writing today, Ibn-Khaldun would replace the word *essences* with genotype. He would be saying: "Nature prepares the genotypes (essences) of species to be transformed into the genotypes of the adjacent species." Similarly, instead of saying "transformed into the next stage by nature," he would say, "Gradual evolution [of life] can be explained in terms of small genetic changes (mutations) in the species and by the ordering of this genetic variation by natural selection."

Close to a millennium before Charles Darwin, Muslims described natural selection. Al-Biruni (973-1048) believed that God delegated active nature (*kiyan*) to perform its assigned duties in the universe. He explains natural selection in almost the same words as did Darwin centuries later. He also sees examples of selection in the methods of horticulturists, as well as in the natural behavior of bees. Al-Biruni writes in *Fi Tahqiq Ma Li'l-Hind* (*Al-Biruni's India*):

The agriculturist selects his corn, letting grow as much as he requires, and tearing out the remainder. The forester leaves those branches, which he perceives to be excellent, whilst he cuts away all others. The bees kill those of their kind who only eat, but do not work in their beehive. Nature proceeds in a similar way.[88]

The following quotes from al-Biruni support the idea that, long before Malthus and Darwin, he knew about the disparity between reproduction and survival. He describes here speciation and natural selection as a result of structural advantages in some species of plants and animals. Al-Biruni writes in *Fi Tahqiq Ma Li'l-Hind* (*Al-Biruni's India*):

"The life of the world depends upon sowing and procreating. Both processes increase in the course of time, and this increase is unlimited, while the world is limited. *When a class of plants or animals does not increase any more in its structure, and its peculiar kind is established as species of its own* (italics mine), when each individual of it does not simply come into existence once and perish, but procreates a being like itself or several together, and not only once but several times, then this will, as single species of plants or animals, occupy the earth and spread itself and its kind over as much territory as it can find."[89]

There is little difference in the views of al-Biruni and Darwin. Both agree that organic beings have unlimited ability to procreate, but that the world is limited. And both concur that individual variations in the structure of organic beings determine the survival of the peculiar kind among the species. Although Darwin labels the natural phenomenon as "natural selection," al-Biruni closely describes it when he uses phrases such as "nature proceeds in a similar way."

Western contemporaries of Charles Darwin knew that many Muslim scholars believed in the evolution of life. John William Draper (1812–1883), a prominent scientist, evolutionist, and professor of chemistry at New York University, was a contemporary of Charles Darwin. He was the first president of the American Chemical Society. Six months after the publication of Darwin's book, Professor Draper presented a paper at the meeting for the British Association for the Advancement of Science entitled "The Intellectual Development of Europe Considered with Respect to the Views of Mr. Darwin." During the discussion of this paper, Bishop Wilberforce of Oxford contemptuously inquired of Thomas Huxley, an eminent scientist and advocate of the theory of evolution, whether Huxley claimed his descent from monkeys "through his grandfather or grandmother."[90] Draper pointed out in one of his books, *History of the Conflict between Science and Religion* (1878) that

"[Western] theological authorities were therefore constrained to look with disfavor on any attempt to carry back the origin of the earth to an epoch indefinitely remote, and on the *Mohammedan theory of evolution* (italics mine) which declared that human beings developed over a long period of time from lower forms of life to their present condition."[91]

In the context of the current passionate rejection of the theory of evolution and the demand for equal time for "intelligent design" in science classes by the Religious Right, it is important to know that the theory of evolution was part of the school curriculum in Muslim schools. Draper states:

Sometimes, not without surprise, we meet with ideas which we flatter ourselves with having originated in our own times. *Thus our modern doctrine of evolution and development were taught in their* [Muslim] *schools* (italics mine). In fact they carried them much farther than we are disposed to do, extending them even to inorganic or mineral things.[92]

We have substantiated the pre-Darwin Islamic acknowledgement of the evolution of simple life into human species and the operation of the natural selection in the evolutionary process. How, then, did the medieval Judeo-Christian belief that God created Eve from Adam's rib become a part of the Muslim faith? Ibn-Khaldun maintains that the sources for this story can be traced back to early Muslims, contemporaries of the Prophet Muhammad and to men who belonged to the generation that succeeded him. According to him, records preserved by these men involved both reliable and unreliable materials. The reason for that, according to Ibn-Khaldun, is that the early Arabs had no books or scholarship [and] desert attitude and illiteracy prevailed among them. When they wanted to learn certain things that human beings are usually curious to know, such as the reasons for existing things, the beginning of creation, and secrets of existence, they consulted earlier People of the Book (Jews and Christians).

Ibn-Khaldun maintains that when these men converted to Islam, they clung to some of their Judeo-Christian beliefs, such as the beginning of creation. He acknowledges that converts such as Ka'b ul-ahbar, Wahb ibn Munabbiah, Abdullah Ibn Slam, and others "filled the Qur'anic commentaries with such materials, which originated . . . with the people of the Torah," and therefore such information was neither sound nor verifiable. In Ibn-Khaldun's view, their interpretations were accepted because they were "people of rank in [their] religion and religious community." In the light of the testimony of Ibn-Khaldun, one of Islam's greatest historiographers and a devout Muslim, we can see that Muslims incorporated the story of the creation of Eve from Adam's rib not through the authority of the Qur'an, but through information they acquired from Jewish and Christian converts.[93] There is no Qur'anic, historical, or scientific basis to accept the contemporary Muslim belief of the *ex nihilo* creation of Adam and the creation of Eve from Adam's rib.

The following verse is used by many Muslims to discredit the acknowledgment of Adam and Eve only as spiritual parents, not DNA–based parents: "O mankind! Lo! We have created you from a male and female, and have made you nations and tribes."(Qur'an 49:13)[94]

According to Zamakhshari (d. 1144)[95] and Al-Razi (1149–1209),[96] the phrase "created from a male and female" have two different meanings depending on the reader. For Muslims who believe in the origin of the human species from Adam and Eve as told originally in the book of Genesis, the phrase means Adam and Eve as the original parents of humankind. The other meaning is that every human born on the earth has a father and mother. Unlike the common contemporary Muslim interpretation of Adam and Eve being primordial parents, the second interpretation does not contradict the divine law of population bottleneck, and so the human species is preserved from extinction. The human material body functions only as a high-tech robotic arm for the human soul to accomplish his/her intentions and plans in the material world. When human intentions, ambitions, and ideas are transcribed into a material medium by the use of his/her material body, similar minded humans (souls) join together and build walls around them to form tribes, nations, cults, religions, etc. That is what we experience in real life; that is what is meant by the above verse 49:13.

The following verse supplements this explanation.

"Mankind was but one community; then they differed; and had it not been for a word that had already gone forth from thy Lord it had been judged between them in respect of that wherein they differ." (Qur'an 10:19)[97]

Within the context of the Qur'an, the very first known organized nation or human community was under the guidance of the Prophet Adam. Islam was the guiding principle for the community. Later, they "differed" and formed "nations and tribes." Therefore, the argument against the theory of evolution rooted in verse 43:12 from the Qur'an is refuted.

The Problem of Chance and the Qur'an

One can find many points of harmony between modern science, the Qur'an, and the early Muslim scholars. Unlike materialist scientists, who proclaim that there is no purpose for the universe, the world's major religions stress that God created the universe by design and for a purpose. The Prophet Muhammad explains it as follows: "God said: I was a hidden treasure. I wanted to be known, so I created the world."[98] Therefore, creatures who know God worship Him by their free choice. Worship means acceptance of divine guidance and acting upon it righteously. God told also that His creatures are accountable on the Day of Judgment for their actions in the current material universe. The divine gift of limited free will is contingent upon individual accountability. The presence of free will demands co-existent multiple choices and the chance to choose any of the available choices. Therefore, chance or random events become essential components of Islam as they are for the theory of evolution.

However, many Muslims believe that assigning a role for chance in the creation is anti-Islamic, a denial of God's absolute control of the universe. Their argument against chance events in nature conflicts with common sense and the Qur'an. In their view, the universe is like a clock and God is the clockmaker. The clockmaker set the clock in motion to tick away toward the Day of Judgment. This miraculous clock never slows down, never runs fast, and never stops. A perfect clock! But if the universe does run like a clock, then future events should be precisely predictable.

If the universe is a mechanical clock whose function was predetermined in the past, all God could do is helplessly observe it ticking away to the end of the universe. We would have an unemployed God! A universe without chance and variety of possibilities exists only if creatures do not have the potential or freedom to help or to hurt, to believe or not to believe in God, and so on. In a deterministic, chance-absent universe, humans cannot choose freely what they want, but are forced to submit to destiny, and God is responsible for unthinkable evils. In the predestined universe posited by anti-evolutionists, our thoughts and resulting deeds are preordained by the clockmaker. But if this were so—if God prompts every move of His earthly creatures—genuine tests or trials as described in the Qur'an on Earth are impossible.

According to the Qur'an, the current universe is only a testing ground for us to gather data in preparation for the Day of Judgment, when God will either reward or punish us based upon His evaluation of what we gathered during our lifetime. The Qur'an states: "[God] Who created death and life in order to try you to see who of you are best in deed," (Qur'an 67:2)[99] and "Or do ye think that you shall enter the Garden [of Bliss] without such [trials] as came to those who passed away before you?" (Qur'an 2:214)[100] It also reads: "On no soul does God place a burden greater than it can bear. It will receive every good it earned and suffer every ill it earned." (Qur'an 2:286)[101] Therefore, in the Islamic universe, every human being is a free agent, given equal chances and the free will to perform moral or immoral acts—equal chances to get to heaven or hell. What each human being does on this earth matters on the Day of Judgment, when the Divine's absolute justice prevails. On the contrary, without the chance to do good or evil, these verses are not meaningful and the Day of Judgment becomes a tyrant's phony court hearing where preprogrammed robots called humans, who have no control over their actions or decisions, are capriciously judged. Without genuine freedom and the chance to do good or evil, the concept of a generous (*Al-Karim*), merciful (*Ar-Rahman*) God is only a fantasy.

There is yet another very important reason against a totally deterministic universe. Most anti-evolutionist Muslims would not deny that God used the elements of chance and unpredictability in the historical processes that produced our contemporary universe and human history. They cannot deny this fact, because the revelation of many Qur'anic verses emerged as a direct answer to the free human choices of the Prophet and his contemporaries. A marvelous example is

the revelation of the first ten verses of chapter 80, "He Frowned (*Abasa*)."
One day the Prophet was engrossed in a conversation with some of the
most influential chieftains of pagan Mecca, hoping to convince them of
the divine message. At that point, a blind ordinary man approached him
with the request for an elucidation of certain earlier verses of the Qur'an.
Annoyed by this interruption of what he momentarily regarded as a
more important endeavor, Prophet Muhammad "frowned and turned
away" from the blind man. Immediately, there and then, the first ten
verses of chapter 80 (He Frowned) were revealed through the angel
Gabriel to reprove the Prophet's treatment of the blind man. The verses
read:

He frowned and turned away, Because a blind man came to him.
What made you think that he [blind man] will not grow in virtue, Or
be admonished, and the admonition profit him? As for him who is
not in want of anything, You pay full attention, Though it is not your
concern if he should not grow (in fullness). As for him who come to
you striving (after goodness) . . . (Qur'an 1-8)[102]

If chance exists in the daily affairs of human beings and even of the
Prophet and shapes their histories and epics, even their religions and
holy books including the Qur'an, there is no reason for Muslims to reject
the role of chance in shaping our biological history. We can discern no
reason to reject the integration of chance or random events with the
evolution of life.

How did God design and direct this miraculous universe yet allow
for chance and random events? What are its mechanics? How does God
respond to and answer prayers without violating natural laws? How
does He maintain the continuity and directionality in the evolution of the
universe and life in the presence of chance? In order to answer these
questions, the Qur'anic concepts of (1) the structure of the material
universe; (2) the self and subjectivity in animate and inanimate beings;
and (3) the often-repeated Muslim phrase, *Inshah Allah* (God so will) are
to be explained.

Materialists say that the universe is not intelligently designed. Herein,
however, we explore the structure of the universe as a product of an
intelligent master design to serve the purpose and intent of God in the
presence of free will in His creatures. In the hands of Niels Bohr,
quantum theory melted solid matter—the basic building material of the
universe and its contents (including humans)—into nonsolid energy.
According to the theory, the more accurately we measure the
momentum, the less accurately we can calculate the position of a particle.
The more we know about the particle's position, the less we can say
about its momentum. Our partial information about the position of a
particle only yields the probability that it is within a certain distance of a

particular point. This scientific paradox bothered even Einstein, who nonetheless concluded, "God does not play dice." However, the physical evidence for quantum reality was overwhelming, leading Neils Bohr to ask, "Who is Einstein to tell God what to do?" Thus we see that the physical sciences cannot tell us when an event will take place, and sometimes it cannot even predict what will happen. If science cannot tell us what is occurring with matter, the basic building material of the universe and living organisms, how can it precisely predict the future of human beings or anything else in the universe? The formation and maintenance of the structure of compounds such as DNA are ultimately the result of phenomena determined by quantum mechanics, where the behavior of atoms is predictable only as a statistical average. Every thought and every motion of all life forms are inseparably connected to electricity and chemistry, and ultimately with unpredictable quantum events. Thus, twentieth-century relativity and quantum mechanics overturned and swept aside the concept of a predetermined universe and replaced it with an indeterminate universe.

Based upon the modern theories, Brown University biologist Kenneth R. Miller points out that God made the larger components of the universe comprehensible to the human mind, the most complex of His creations, with the installation of inflexible, reliable chemical and physical laws to function in a uniform and repetitive fashion at the level of those larger components. However, God created the atomic and sub-atomic world to function in an unpredictable fashion. If the atomic world were functioning in a uniform and predictable fashion, then we would be able to foresee the future accurately through our knowledge of past causes. If this were the case, humankind would lose its freedom to make moral choices. God would then be restricted to the role of a passive spectator, unable to act without suspending the laws of the universe in a way that is visibly obvious to humans.[103] Therefore, God created matter as the building material of the universe and had it governed by an immutable system of physical and chemical laws within which matter functions in unpredictable ways. By doing so, He granted human beings the freedom to make moral choices about their future. Due to the built-in unpredictability in the structure of matter, we will not have absolute knowledge of the nature and future of our universe until the Day of Judgment.

This construction of understandable chemistry coupled with unpredictable quantum physics is an ingenious intelligent design of the All Knowing and All Powerful God. Within this master design of the universe, God gave His creatures a genuine freedom and an open future, while at the same time giving humans the ability to derive sensible meanings out of the complex universe. In such a material universe, God can, in response to His creatures' prayers, intervene in the universe by causing small quantum events without suspending the understandable laws of classical chemistry and physics. Similarly, in such a design of the universe, God has the freedom to create any being or substance, living or nonliving, without disturbing any laws of classical physics and chemistry, by making a quantum event in the atomic world. In this material universe, therefore, God does play dice between the big bang and the big crunch to create free will for His creatures.

Self and Subjectivity in the Inanimate World

According to science, life is a condition that distinguishes living organisms from inorganic objects and dead organisms. In the Qur'anic universe, such a distinction is blurred, and not only animate but also inorganic objects are alive; God endowed all creatures with mind. Inanimate entities, such as fire, wind and mountains, have self and a subjective faculty with which they can experience and respond to the Divine Will. However, human beings do not comprehend it: "The seven skies, the earth, and all that lies within them, sing praise to Him. And there is nothing that does not chant His praise. But you [human] do not understand their hymns of praise." (Qur'an 17:44)[104] We also read: "Then he turned to the heavens, and it was smoke. So he said to the earth and the heavens: Come with willingness and obedience and they replied: We come willingly." (Qur'an 41:11)[105] The Qur'anic verses here describe a universe that has been responsive to God since its inception after the big bang. The heavens and the earth in its early gaseous embryonic state ("smoke") respond to God by saying, "We come willingly." Then, God offered the heavens, earth and the mountains the opportunity to bear the responsibility of carrying out His will, giving them the choice to deviate from it at the risk of punishment. They refused because they were afraid of violating it and of punishment. The verse reads: "Surely We presented the trust to the heavens and the earth, and the mountains, but they declined to bear it and they feared it, and man bore it, but he is iniquitous, ignorant." (Qur'an 33:72)[106]

In the Qur'anic universe, natural events such as thunder, fire, and wind have self and subjectivity: "And the thunder extols His praise, and the angels are in of awe of Him." (Qur'an 13:13)[107] The subjectivity of fire is well documented in the verses. When Abraham was cast into fire, God said: "Turn cold, O fire, and give safety to Abraham." (Qur'an 21:69)[108] A verse relating to Solomon reads: "So We subjected the wind to him [Solomon]; it ran softly at his command to wherever he pleased." (Qur'an 38:36)[109] Like fire, thunder, etc., having assigned duties and functions, "and He assigned to each heaven its duties and command." (Qur'an

41:12)[110] Even a simple shadow of any object has self and subjectivity, and worships God: "Have they not seen . . . their shadows . . . prostrating themselves before God in all servility?" (Qur'an 16:48)[111] These verses guided Jalaluddin Rumi (1207-1273), a celebrated Muslim mystic poet, to write his *Masnavi*: "Air and earth and water and fire are [His] slaves. With you and me they are dead, but with thy God they are alive."[112]

In the Islamic spiritual dominion, every part of a whole organism has its own inherent individual subjective faculty with which to experience and to respond, and has a separate physical existence from the whole, as we can see from the following verse: "This day (Judgment Day) We seal their mouths, and their hands speak to Us and their feet will bear witness concerning what they earned." (Qur'an 36:65)[113] Another verse warns that on the Day of Judgment "their ears and their eyes and their skins will testify against them as to what they used to do. And they say unto their skins: Why did you testify against us? They say: God, who gave all things power of articulation, made us to speak." (Qur'an 41:20-21)[114] Thus we see that the individual components of organisms, such as their ears, feet, skin, etc., have some measure of feeling that would allow them to respond to the guidance of God. Similarly, DNA and genes, being a part of all organisms, also have independent existences and can respond to God independent of the whole.

A few modern western scientists, for example, the late Alfred N. Whitehead, British mathematician philosopher, and John F. Haught, professor of Theology at Georgetown University, have accepted the presence of subjectivity and inner sense within all life forms—from single cell organisms to the most complex human being. Whitehead accepts subjectivity for inanimate beings also. The inner potential in lower orders of creatures may be minimal and hard to detect. As God created higher orders of being, He carefully gifted each of them with more potential, so they could experience the outside world and be able to understand more complex messages from God. Materialists ridicule the idea of an inner sense with the subjective capacity to experience and respond in inanimate beings. However, no one can explain how an electron jumps from one orbit to another. Ernest Rutherford, a famous physicist, states that an electron would have to "know" beforehand to which orbit it was going to jump. Otherwise, it would not emit light with a single, definite wavelength when it starts its leap.[115]

We acknowledge small and large DNA-based creatures as parts of a greater whole called life. Similarly, inanimate objects such as stars and galaxies, the earth, the continents and subcontinents, states and nations and so on, are atomic aggregates. Environments as tiny as a petri dish with a growth of bacteria in a laboratory, and as huge as North America or Asia, are parts of a whole called nature. All separately identifiable entities in the universe have self and subjectivity. We have seen from Qur'anic verse (16:48) that even the shadow of any object worships and responds to God. Therefore, an environment such as a petri dish, the Galapagos Islands or a continent is alive and has self and subjectivity.

God created varying levels of inner sense and subjectivity with the faculty to experience and respond for whole systems and for their parts. Therefore, when He addresses His creatures, He mercifully expects different levels of response from them. The complexity of information arriving for the use of any hierarchical order of being depends upon that order's inherent level of intellect and capability to actualize the information. Obviously, God did not want an amoeba to fly an airplane, but He wants human beings and *Jinn* to explore the heavens, as clearly revealed in the following verse: "O society of *jinn* and men, cross the bounds of heavens and the earth if you have ability, do then pass beyond them. But you cannot unless you acquire the law." (Qur'an 55:33)[116]

How the presence of the self and subjectivity in all beings affects the evolution of the universe and life can be understood only if we understand the Qur'anic concept of the metaphysics of the future.

The Metaphysics of the Future

Materialist scientists argue that biological evolution is an "inherently mindless purposeless process." Biologist and atheist Richard Dawkins stresses that the unfolding of life is the result of selfish desires of genes to increase their opportunities for survival and reproduction. Richard Lewontin, a Harvard University biologist, steps into an extreme form of scientism when he states, "materialism is absolute [and] we cannot allow a Divine Foot in the door."[117] Such fervency stems from an unshakable, unwavering faith in the Law of Causality, which states that a given cause always produces the same effect. Gravity always pulls an apple down to the earth; the spring season melts snow; drought brings the destruction of crops. Chemical reactions in any organism, amoeba or human, are explainable by the same laws of physics and chemistry that govern the universe. Based on causality, scientists maintain that the future is predetermined and can be predicted through accurate knowledge of past causes. The laws of nature, they argue, are invariant, and scientific observation reveals the past as the product of those laws. Any natural event that departs from the anticipated effect of a uniform cause is classified as an "accident." However, scientists' predictions based on observation of matter and invariant laws of nature are limited by their own earlier conclusions and experiences.

To gather data, scientists peer into nature, from atoms to stars, amoebas to humankind, fungi to maple trees, and any other phenomena of our universe. Science has categorized the collected data, defining disciplines such as paleontology, comparative anatomy, biogeography, embryology, molecular genetics, and so on. The materialists' claim that the unfolding of life is a "purposeless, mindless process" is based upon inferences from separately catalogued extrapolations of past experiences. John F. Haught calls such materialistic metaphysics "metaphysics of the past."[118] Haught's outstanding treatise *God After Darwin* helped me develop a better understanding of Islam and the concept of Creation described in the Qur'an. I find his mode of thought to be as much Islamic as his belief system, so I shall apply his metaphysics to an Islamic context. In the Islamic universe, unlike that catalogued by materialist science, the past and the present are not the creators of the future, nor are humans or any other creatures, because "God is the creator of everything." (Qur'an 13:16)[119] Even creations that we claim as our own emanate from God. The Qur'an states, "And God created you and what you make." (Qur'an 37:96)[120] God created everything—computers, airplanes, cars and even the atom.

A few important questions might be asked: If God is the creator of what humans make, is God not also the creator of our good and bad deeds? Why should there be reward for the pious and retribution for the impious on the Day of Judgment if God is the source of our actions? The answer to these questions lies in the Islamic metaphysics of the future derived from the phrase, *Inshah Allah* (God so willing).

In the life of devout Muslims, a day never passes without using the Arabic phrase *Inshah Allah* (God so willing) at the end of any conversation pertaining to the future, even for simple tasks such as meeting a friend at 4 pm tomorrow. Without an understanding of the meaning of this phrase, we cannot begin to comprehend God's relationship with His creatures, the concept of Creation, and the role of free will. Nor can we offer a rational, internally consistent argument against the materialists' exclusion of God in the evolution of life and the universe. Islamic teachings regarding the coming of future events are grounded in the verse, "And never say about anything, 'Behold, I shall do this tomorrow,' without [adding] 'if God so wills.' " (Qur'an 18:23)[121] Muslims believe that the *future* is not simply born without cause. It occurs only when and if God creates it. Future means the yet-to-be-born or created moment packed with contrasting or diametrically opposite possibilities as information. The experienced past is irretrievable; the present is only a fleeting moment that we cannot hold. On the other hand, we experience the continuous coming of the future.

Moments of the future are messenger moments that carry information and proposals from God to His creatures. Each moment brings each of us hope or fear, success or failure, pain or pleasure, routine or surprise events. However, the information enclosed in the messenger moments has neither negative nor positive value until creatures actualize it in the material form. As we learned earlier, in the Qur'anic universe, all separately identifiable components and forces have self and subjectivity, and can respond to God. If and when the creatures act upon the information and proposals, transcribing them into visible realities of material media, we recognize these visible realities as the monuments of divine creations. Our planning and our desires may or may not be what God is going to present to us in our future. God states: "and they contrived, and God contrived, but God is the greatest of contrivers." (Qur'an 3:54)[122] To label the above belief, we shall borrow John F. Haught's phrase "metaphysics of the future" [123] and modify it to read "Islamic metaphysics of the future." If a future moment arrives lacking in novel possibilities, humans and other creatures cannot change their present condition, which then becomes stagnant and may remain so for an unlimited period of time. Even when God sends our way moments with novel possibilities, we will remain unchanged if we do not accept His offerings and revelations.

Nothing comes into existence without the information about it being initially available. Information comes out of scientific laboratories almost daily. Those who understand the information can then transform it into cars, airplanes, nations and so on. A metaphor of the factory worker illustrates our relationship to God. While the ordinary assembly-line worker can choose the manufacturing plant in which he wishes to be employed, factory workers have no freedom to manufacture any products of their choice; they must assemble a product using components coming through the conveyer belt of the factory.

The physical and spiritual universe is the manufacturing plant of Islam owned by God, the supreme Scientist and Technician. Here creatures at large, and humans in particular, are like assembly- line workers. The chain of flowing moments of the coming future is the conveyer belt, which delivers the raw materials (possibilities as information) necessary for the making of many products. In this factory the worker is free to select any of the components (possibilities) from the conveyer belt (arriving future) and actualize those possibilities into visible monuments of God's creation. If there is no flow of information from scientists and technicians, the assembly-line worker is unable to produce anything. Even the factory would not exist. Likewise, humans or any other creatures cannot produce or act upon the world until the future moment arrives with possibilities as information from God. Therefore, in Islamic metaphysics of the future, the universe is always within God's providence. Therefore, God is the creator of all things and the one who sends messenger moments that carry His proposals. Consequently, individuals opt to receive reward or retribution in the hereafter universe based upon their earthly choices.

The universe from the big bang to the big crunch is a maze. On both ends, there is a singularity where all matter is condensed into a mathematical point. The maze is made out of alleys, roads, highways and byways that lead to different futures for the universe and its components. God has already mapped out all the possible and available futures that we can choose, but it is still up to humans and other components of the universe, day by day or moment by moment, to decide for themselves which alleys or roads or highways to step into. God, the Merciful and Benevolent, does not interfere or force us into making choices. So, as the Qur'an states: Whoso interveneth in a good cause will have the reward thereof; and whoso interveneth in an evil cause will bear the consequence thereof. God overseeth all things. (4:85)[124]

God knows that free will would be nonexistent for His creatures without limitation of His omnipotence and omniscience. Creatures would not be able to choose when the future arrives with possibilities from God without voluntary self-limitation of His power and absolute knowledge. Therefore, *Al-Rahman* (The Beneficient) and *Al-Rahim* (The Merciful) God sets a voluntarily self-imposed limitation on His omniscience and omnipotence to create free will for His creatures as stated in the Qur'anic verse: "And had your Lord willed, whoever in the earth would have believed altogether. Will you then coerce the people to become believers?" (Qur'an 10:99)[125] The self-imposed limitation being voluntary, it does not imply any inherent limitation in God's ultimate power and omniscience. At the same time we are free to choose and actualize any of the worldly possibilities available to us—atomic power, computer technology, biological engineering—but our future is limited by the possibilities that God has in store for us. In another words, God knows all available futures for creatures, but in order to create free will for His creatures, God, being the Most Merciful and Most Benevolent, voluntarily opted not to know which future path His creatures would choose to step into until it is done.

Based upon the teachings of the Qur'an, the far-reaching meaning of the phrase *Inshah Allah* (God so willing), and the concept of Islamic metaphysics of the future, new species are born when previously existing beings truly grasp and actualize the novel proposals enclosed within imminent moments delivered by God. Haught describes this evolutionary metaphysics of the future most elegantly and clearly: "Evolution happens, ultimately, because of the 'coming of God' [with His proposals] towards the entire universe from out of an elusive future."[126] We see that, while evolutionary accidents or contingencies appear random, they come from God as novel suggestions. The pivotal moment called "the present" is the opening into the material world. When messenger moments with novel possibilities or potentialities arrive at this door and when a creature objectifies them, we may see a mutation or the birth of a new species. An event in nature may appear random to humans, because we have no knowledge of what each messenger moment of the future has brought to every creature in the universe, and we also have no means to know what every individual being has chosen to objectify into monuments of divine creation.

By granting freedom to His creatures to choose from His proposals contained in the arriving messenger moments of the future, God distances Himself from being a tyrant and distinguishes Himself as the All Merciful (ar-Rahman) and The Evolver (al-Baari). He only proposes, and creatures dispose. The final result is that we live in a dynamic universe that is alive and being created at every moment in the dazzling dance between God's limited creatures and His unlimited imagination.

Within the Islamic metaphysics of the future, the universe is always under God's providence and never leaves His hand because He has the absolute power and free will to decide what possibilities to offer us. This providence is reflected in the verse,

Extol the limitless glory of thy Rabb (Evolver): [the glory of] the All-Highest, who creates [everything], and thereupon forms it in accordance with what it is meant to be, and who determines the nature [of all that exists], and thereupon guides it [towards its fulfillment]. (Qur'an 87:1–3)[127]

Guidance in the verse means the divine proposals delivered through the messenger moments as well as His divine books. Humans as well as all other separately identifiable subunits of the universe have the freedom based upon individual competency to choose and actualize the offered possibilities into visible monuments of God's creation. In such an unpredictable universe, some get hurt while others prosper. Jalaluddin Rumi describes the scenario in Masnavi as follows:

The Universe, when you look at it closely, presents a universal struggle—atom struggling with atom like faith against infidelity. The struggle in action is the objective form of the principle of opposition, which has its basis in their inner nature. There is war in words and war in deeds and war in nature; between the parts of the Universe there is a terrible war. This war is the very constitution of the Universe; look into the elements and you understand it. Creation is based on opposition; therefore, every creature became warlike to get some benefit and avoid some injury. Because without need Almighty God does not give anything to anyone; if there were no necessity, the seven heavens would not have stepped out of nonexistence; the sun and the moon and the stars could not have come into existence without necessity; so necessity is the cause of all existence, and according to his necessity man is endowed with organs. Therefore, O needy one, Increase your need so that God's beneficence may be moved [to bestow new instruments of life on me].[128]

Scientists who deny the existence of God do not see any purpose or function for the universe. They reject an intelligent design of the universe because the organisms we see in nature show evidence of either bad design or suboptimal design. From a physician's point of view, for example, humans walking around on hind legs causes problems ranging from back pain to hemorrhoids, and the vestigial organ the appendix only makes us sick. So their assessment seems to make sense when looking at the universe through an atheistic prism. Contrary to their inference, most God-conscious people, including Muslims, believe the universe was intelligently designed for a divine purpose. We observe intelligent design in a product only if it perfectly serves the purpose for which it is crafted. Therefore, unless we have a general idea regarding the product's purpose, it is humanly impossible to know whether the product is intelligently designed. So, what is the purpose of the universe as viewed through the Muslim prism? We have seen earlier that "God said: I was a hidden treasure. I wanted to be known, so I created the world." In order to know Him, He gave us guidance through His holy Books written in human vernacular and the universe written in material media. According to the Qur'an Verse 6:32, "This world's life is but jest and frolic. Better surely for those who fear God, will be the last abode. Do you not then comprehend?"[129] and Verse 2:155-156: "And surely We shall test you with something of fear and hunger, and loss of wealth and lives and crops; yet give good tidings to the patient, who, when affliction strikes them, say, 'Surely we belong to God, and to Him shall we return.'"[130] Therefore, our current universe is only a temporary abode for trial before admission to the eternal hereafter world of absolute peace and bliss is granted. Unlike the perfect hereafter world of absolute happiness and bliss, the defects in the components of the universe are built into it to make the trial efficient and possible. In fact, trial is impossible in a perfect world without pain and suffering from death and destruction. Therefore, our current short-living universe may be imperfect structurally, but it has a perfect structure to function as a testing ground. As such, our current universe is intelligently designed to serve God's plan and purpose.

Conclusion

Although many contemporary Muslims believe that God instantaneously created the human species, science has shown that life on Earth evolved over billions of years. Similarly, many Muslims in their classical period believed that creation is a process that occurred over a long period of earthly time. Based upon the Qur'an, all separately identifiable animate and inanimate entities in the material world are God's creatures. All have self, subjectivity and feelings. When creatures experience divine proposals brought by the arriving messenger moments of the future and selectively transcribe them into material media, the future becomes visible monuments of divine creation. Yet, stunningly, in this potentially chaotic universe, which evolves through the practice of free choice by an infinite number of creatures, order emerges. Such order results from the interplay between the organization of proposals that God makes within messenger moments and the choices creatures make, based on their self-interest. Our miraculous universe, that blends creation, an infinite number of creatures with feelings, messenger moments, and the cumulative moment-by-moment transcriptions of the chosen divine proposals into material media by entire creatures together, appears to be evolving as described by the theories of evolution of life and the universe. What an amazing intelligent construction of the universe by the One and the Only Amazing Compassionate God! Yet, "No vision can grasp Him, but His grasp is over all vision: He is above all comprehension, yet is acquainted with all things." (Qur'an: 6:103)[131]

NOTES

1. Pickthall, Mohammed Marmaduke. 1930. *Holy Qur'an*. Hyderbad, India: H. E. H. Mir Osman Ali Khan. Verse 21:104.

2. Nooruddin, Allammah. 2001. *The Holy Qur'an*. Hockenssin, Delaware: Inc. Noor Foundation. Verses 55:5–9.

3. Ibid 20:53–54.

4. Khathib, M. M. 1984. *The Bounteous Koran*. London: Macmillan Press, Verses 3:190–191.

5. Ali, Maulana Muhammad. 1991. *The Holy Qur'an*. Columbus, OH: Ahmadiyyah Anjuman Isha'at Islam. Verse 29:20.

6. Khathib. M.M. *The Bounteous Koran*. Verse 67: 3.

7. Ibid. Verses 51:20–21.

8. Al-Ghazzali, Imam Abu-Hamid. (1058–1111) *Ihya Ulum-Id-Din*. Translated by Al-Haj Maulana Fazal-Ul-Karim. Lahore.Pakistan: Book Lovers Bureau, 1971. Vol. 1, 20–21.

9. Ali, Ahmed. 1990. *Al-Qur'an*. Princeton: Princeton University Press. Verse 21:30.

10. Ibid. Verse 41:11.

11. Asad, Muhammad. 1980. *The Message of the Qur'an*. Gibraltar: Dar Al-Andalus. Qur'an 51:47.

12. Ibid. 491.

13. Al-Biruni. (d. 1048) *The Athar-Ul-Bakiya* (*The Chronology of Ancient Nations*). Translated by Dr. C. Edward Sachu. 1879. London: W. H. Allen. 30.

14. Al-Biruni. *Kitab Tahdid al-Amakin Listashiah Masafat al-Masakin* (*The Determination of the Coordinates of Positions for Correction of Distances between Cities*). Translated by Jamil Ali. 1967. Beirut: The American University of Beirut. 16.

15. Ali, Yusuf. 1977. *The Holy Qur'an*. Indianapolis: American Trust Publications. Verse 46:3.

16. Davies, Paul. 1983. *God and the New Physics*. Simon and Schuster, Inc. 204.

17. Ali, Ahmed, *Al-Qur'an*. Verse 81:15.

18. Sagan, Carl. 1980. *Cosmos*. New York: Random House. 267. Arberry, Arthur J. *The Koran Interpreted*. New York: Collier Books, Verse 81:1.

19. Ibid 78:8.

20. Pickthall, Mohammed Marmaduke. *Holy Qur'an*. 75:9.

21. Ali, Yusuf. *The Holy Qur'an*. Verse 52:6 Arberry 81:6.

22. Davies, Paul. 1983. *God and the New Physics*. Simon and Schuster, Inc.

23. Arberry, Arthur J. *The Koran Interpreted*. Verse 81:6.

24. Davies, Paul. 1983. *God and the New Physics*. Simon and Schuster, Inc. 204.

25. Salahi, Adil. M.and Ashur A. Shamis. 1979. *In the Shade of the Qur'an*. Verses 81:11.

26. Ali, Yusuf. Verse 25:25.

27. Ibid. Verse 69:14.

28. Ibid. Verse 82:1–2.

29. Ibid. Verse 81:2.

30. Ibid. Verse 55:37.

31. Ibid. Verse 55:37.

32. Sagan, Carl. *Cosmos*. 267.

33. Dawood, N. J. 1990. *The Koran*. New York: Penguin Books. Verse 21:104.

34. Ibid Verse 14:48.

35. Maududi, Abul A'la S. 1984. *The Meaning of the Qur'an*. Lahore, Pakistan: Islamic Publications (Pvt.) Ltd. Verse 79:46.

36. Asad, Muhammad. *The Message of the Qur'an*. Verse 10:45.

37. Ali, Yusuf. *The Holy Qur'an*. Verse 4:82.

38. Asad, Muhammad. *The Message of the Qur'an*. Verse 96:1–2.

39 Azad, Mawlana Abdul Kalam. *Tarjuman al-Qur'an*. Translated by Syed Abdul Latif. Hyderabad, India. 1981 Dr. Syed Abdul Latif's Trust for Qur'anic and other Cultural Studies. 19.

40. Ali, Maulana Muhammad. 1950. *The Religion of Islam*. Lahore, Pakistan: Ahmadiyyah Anjuman Ish'at Islam. 135.

41. Lane, Edward William. *Arabic-English Lexicon*. Beirut, Lebanon: Libraire Du Liban, 1980. Part 2, 799–800.

42. Ali, Yusuf. *The Holy Qur'an*. Verse 59:24.

43. Lane, Edward William. *Arabic-English Lexicon*. Part 1, 178.

44. Lane, Edward William. *Arabic-English Lexicon*. Part 4, 1745.

45. Khathib, M. M. *The Bounteous Koran*. Verse 19:19.

46. Ali, Yusuf. *The Holy Qur'an*. Verse 10:4.

47. Ali, Yusuf. *The Holy Qur'an*. 484.

48. Lane, Edward William. *Arabic-English Lexicon*. Part 3, 1142.

49. Ali, Yusuf. *The Holy Qur'an*. Verse 32:7.

50. Bucaille, Maurice. 1983. *What is the Origin of Man?* Paris, France: Seghers. 173.

51. Edward William. *Arabic-English Lexicon*. Part 6, 2350.

52. Khathib, M. M. *The Bounteous Koran*. Verse 64:3.

53. Asad, Muhammad. *The Message of the Qur'an*. Verse 71:14.

54. Gould, Stephen Jay. 1977. *Ever Since Darwin*. New York, London: W. W. Norton. 61.

55. Arberry, Arthur J. 1955. *The Koran interpreted*. New York: Collier Books. Verse 76:1.

56. Hakim, Dr Khalifa Abdul. 1977. *The Metaphysics of Rumi*. Lahore, Pakistan: Institute of Islamic Culture. 36.

57. Ali, Yusuf. *The Holy Qur'an*. Verse. 23:12.

58. http://www.origins.rpi.edu/chem.html.

59. Khathib, M. M. *The Bounteous Koran*. Verse 1:30.

60. Ali, Yusuf. *The Holy Qur'an*. Verse 24:45.

61. Lane, Edward William. *Arabic-English Lexicon*. Part 3, 842.

62. Ibn-Khaldun, Abdul-Rahman (d. 1406). *Muqaddimah*. Translated by Franz Rosenthal. 1980. Princeton: Princeton University Press. Vol. 2, 424.

63. Khathib, M. M. *The Bounteous Koran*. Verses 82:6–7.

64. Pickthall, Mohammed Marmaduke. *Holy Qur'an*. 7:11.

65. Lane, Edward William. *Arabic-English Lexicon*. Part 5, 1973.

66. Arberry, Arthur J. *The Koran interpreted*. Verse 6:133.

67. Lane, Edward William. *Arabic-English Lexicon*. Part 8, 2791.

68. Razi, Fakr al-Din (1149-1209). Lebanon: Dar al-Fikar. *Al Tafsir al-Kabir*. Vol. 7, 212.

69. Lane, Edward William. *Arabic-English Lexicon*. Part 2, 792.

70. Khathib, M. M. *The Bounteous Koran*. Verse 4:1.

71. Ali, Ahmed, *Al-Qur'an*. Verse 39:4.

72. Bukhari, Muhammad ibn Ismail al-Jufi. (d. 897). *Sahih Al-Bukhari*. Translated by Muhammd Muhsin Khan. 1977. Chicago: Khazi

Publications. Vol 8, Book 77, Number 593.

73. Khathib, M. M. *The Bounteous Koran*. Verse 35:65.

74. Pickthall, Mohammed Marmaduke. *Holy Qur'an*. Verses 41:20–21.

75. Ali, Ahmed, *Al-Qur'an*. Verses 75: 3–4.

76. Ibid. Verse 15:29.

77. Ibid. Verse 2:31.

78. Ali, Yusuf. *The Holy Qur'an*. Verse 3:19.

79. Ali, Ahmed, *Al-Qur'an*. Verse 2:136.

80. Arberry, Arthur J. *The Koran interpreted*. 3:67.

81. Shakir. http://www.al-islam.org/quran/ Verses 7:10–11.

82. Ali, Yusuf. *The Holy Qur'an*. Verses 2:35–36.

83. Hussani, S. A. Q. 1979. *The Pantheistic Monism of Ibn Arabi*. Lahore, Pakistan: SH. Muhammad Ashraf. 61–107.

84. Ibn-Khaldun, Abdul-Rahman. *Muqaddimah*. Translated by Franz Rosenthal. Vol. 1, 195.

85. Ibn-Khaldun, Abdul-Rahman. *Muqaddimah*. Translated by Franz Rosenthal. Vol. 3, 238.

86. Ibn-Khaldun, Abdul-Rahman. *Muqaddimah*. Translated by Franz Rosenthal. Vol. 1, 173.

87. Ibn-Khaldun, Abdul-Rahman. *Muqaddimah*. Translated by Franz Rosenthal. Vol. 2, 422–423.

88. Al-Biruni. (d. 1048) *Fi Tahqiq Ma Li'l-Hind* (*Alberuni's India*). Translated by Dr. Edward C. Sachu. 1914. London: Kegan Paul, Trench, Trubner & Co. Ltd. 400.

89. Al-Biruni. (d. 1048) *Fi Tahqiq Ma Li'l-Hind* (*Alberuni's India*). Translated by Dr. Edward C. Sachu. 400.

90. Gould, Stephen Jay. "Knight Takes Bishop?" *Natural History*, May, 1986: 18–33.

91. Draper, John William. 1875. *The Conflict between Religion and Science*. New York: D. Appleton and Company, 187–188.

92. Ibid. 118.

93. Ibn-Khaldun, Abdul-Rahman (d. 1406). *Muqaddimah*. Vol. 2, 444–446.

94. Ali, Yusuf. *The Holy Qur'an*. Verse 49:13.

95. Zamakhshari, Mahmoud ibn Omar (d. 1133). *Al-Kashaf* (Arabic). Lebanon: Dar al-Arabi. 1987. Vol. 4, 374.

96. Razi, Fakr al-Din (1149–1209). *Al Tafsir al-Kabir*. (Arabic). Lebanon: Dar al-Fikar. 1985. Vol. 18, 136–137.

97. Ali, Yusuf. *The Holy Qur'an*. Verse 10:19.

98. Nasr, Seyyed Hussein. 1991. Introduction, in *Islamic Spirituality Foundations*. New York: The Crossroad Publishing Company. xxi.

99. Ali, Ahmed, *Al-Qur'an*. Verse 67:2.

100. Ali, Yusuf. *The Holy Qur'an*. Verse 2:214.

101. Ibid. Verse 2:286.

102. Ali, Ahmed, *Al-Qur'an*. Verse 80: 1–9.

103. Miller, Kenneth. 1999. *Finding Darwin's God*. New York: HarperCollins Publishers Inc.

104. Ali, Ahmed, *Al-Qur'an*. Verse 17: 44.

105. Khathib, M. M. *The Bounteous Koran*. Verse 41:11.

106. Ibid. Verse 33:72.

107. Ibid. Verse 13:13.

108. Ibid. Verse 21:69.

109. Ibid. Verse 38:36.

110. Ibid. Verse 41:12.

111. Ibid. Verse 16:48.

112. Hakim, Dr Khalifa Abdul. *The Metaphysics of Rumi*. 36.

113. Khathib, M. M. *The Bounteous Koran*. Verse 36:65.

114. Ibid. Verse 41:20–21.

115. Morris, Richard. 1988. The Nature of Reality. New York: Noonday Press. 15.

116. Ali, Ahmed, *Al-Qur'an*. Verse 55:33.

117. Richard Lewontin. Book Review of *The Demon-Haunted World: Science as a Cradle in the Dark* by Carl Sagan. *New York Review of Books*, January 9, 1997.

118. Haught, John F. 1999. *God After Darwin*. Boulder: Westview Press. 86.

119. Khathib, M. M. *The Bounteous Koran*. Verse 13:16.

120. Ibid. Verse 37:96.

121. Ibid. Verse 18:23.

122. Ibid. Verse 3:54.

123. Haught, John F. *God After Darwin*. 83–88.

124. Pickthall, Mohammed Marmaduke. *Holy Qur'an*. 4:85.

125. Khathib, M. M. *The Bounteous Koran*. Verse 10:99.

126. Haught, John F. *God After Darwin*. 99.

127. Asad, Muhammad. *The Message of the Qur'an*. Verses 87:1–3.

128. Hakim, Dr Khalifa Abdul. *The Metaphysics of Rumi*. 30.

129. Khathib, M. M. *The Bounteous Koran*. Verse 6:32.

130. Ibid. Verse 2:155–156.

131. Ali, Yusuf. *The Holy Qur'an*. Verse 6:103.

Part Four

Reconciling Scientific Understanding with Religious Faith

I see no good reasons why the views given in *On the Origin of Species* should shock the religious feelings of anyone.
—Charles Darwin

Don't Shoot the Messenger

Yet the first bringer of unwelcome news Hath but a losing office, and his tongue

Sounds ever after as a sullen bell, Remembered knolling a departing friend.
—*King Henry the Fourth*, Part II, Act I, scene 1, line 100

Though it be honest, it is never good To bring bad news.
—*Antony and Cleopatra* Act II, scene 5, line 85

Which came first: religion or science? Religion, because at first, humans wondered who they were and whence they came and answered these questions through deep thought and logic, but without any empiricism. Religion came first and became "established" over thousands of years.

It's been only a few hundred years since humans began to inquire more critically and test their ideas experimentally, refining or rejecting them according to scientific evidence. The theory of evolution, which was thrust upon the collective conscious relatively recently, was a shock to established systems.

In Parts Two and Three, the three religious scientists have reexamined some of those ancient and established religious systems through the lens of modern science. To understand the perspectives from which these scientists have reexamined their religious insights, it is helpful to understand the respective goals and methods of scientific and religious endeavors.

Scientific endeavors are conscientious or concerted efforts toward understanding and explaining the universe. Science attempts as much as possible to base its understandings and explanations (hypotheses, laws, theories, and models) on objectively verifiable experiences. In other words, they are demonstrable (publicly verifiable).

Science supports its ideas with evidence. For science, absolute certainty is unattainable, since subsequent experiments may provide evidence for new insights. Science thus offers proof with as much certainty as possible.

Religious endeavors are also conscientious or concerted efforts toward understanding and explaining the universe. Religious understandings and explanations are not, however, based solely on objectively verifiable experiences. They are also based on subjective experiences (personal experiences that are often shared with others). Such experiences include personal revelations as well as events that many religious people believe transcend the laws of nature (miracles). Religion thus offers certainty without proof (faith).

According to Ashley Montagu, the mutual attempts of science and religion to understand the universe respond to the craving to relate oneself to the mysterious forces of the universe and the craving to reveal and to bring into harmonic order something of its mystery. The different criteria on which these understandings are based, however, have led to vastly different understandings of the history and development of the universe. Despite the temptation of some religious people to eradicate these differences by shooting science, the messenger of newer and different understandings, shooting science is both unnecessary and undesirable because the book of Genesis, Qur'an, and theory of evolution scenarios can be reconciled by thoughtfully examining the nature of the evidence supporting science's fourteen-billion-year message and the nature of the texts from which the 10,000-year figure is calculated.

Infallible Holy Scriptures: Books of Truth

Billions of people live in accordance with Holy Scriptures, "divine" revelations that have been codified and transmitted in writing. They fervently believe that such books contain all the truth that faithful people need to live meaningful lives and that this truth is infallible and therefore cannot be questioned.

Many of them are aware of the stark contrast between the less than 10,000-year history of the universe reckoned by literal interpretations of the book of Genesis and Qur'an and science's relatively recent message that our universe has a fourteen-billion year history. In response to this apparent discrepancy, a considerable number of them have determined that one of these scenarios must be rejected in order to adhere to the other.

Because of their absolute reliance on these books for guidance and inspiration, they are understandably wary and suspicious of suggestions that any portion of Scripture is not literally true. They fear that if they acknowledge that one portion is not literally true, they will have to abandon the entire book along with the religious faith that it legitimizes for them. *They have therefore rejected science's message.*

The challenge of persuading people to give up beliefs they hold dear when evidence clearly indicates that they should, is far more difficult than the problem of presenting this evidence clearly and understandably. No one is immune from at least some reluctance to be wrong, to change their mind, to admit serious mistakes, and accept unwelcome findings. This reluctance is, naturally enough, all the more poignant when the stakes are possible loss of ultimate meaning or even eternal damnation. Thus, the subject should be approached with great care and sensitivity, understanding, and patience.

Three Scientists, One Scientific Theory

In Parts Two and Three of this book, a Christian scientist, a Jewish scientist, and a Muslim scientist have explained why they have confidence in the theory of evolution and how they have reconciled that theory with the Scriptures of their faith. In contrast to fundamentalists, they believe that doubt and reason are gifts to be used to gain deeper insight into the tenets of their religion. They are unanimous in their support for science's assertion that the universe is about fourteen billion years old, planet Earth is about five billion years old, and species evolved rather than were created all at once.

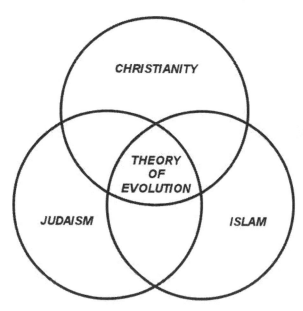

Three Scientists: One Conviction About Whether the Scripture of their Religion is Always Literally True

The scientists are also unanimous in their conviction that not all of their Scriptures should be taken literally. Rabbi Kay and Drs. Shanavas and Van Till have shown that tension between understandings that initially seem inconsistent is relieved once people realize that acceptance of knowledge that became available after the creation of their religious texts does not require them to abandon those texts. The writers' responses testify to the fact that reconciliation is both reasonable and desirable.

Three Scientists: Three Religious Beliefs

Despite being admonished by some religious leaders not to listen to other religious groups' statements about faith, holders of religious beliefs should listen as alertly to descriptions of other beliefs as they hope others will listen to theirs. When they listen, they will, of course, not only recognize areas of common belief, they will also become aware of ways in which the beliefs differ from their own. It is thus no surprise that the three scientists' religious beliefs differ in a number of ways. Understanding and acknowledging these differences can lead to mutual understanding and respect among faiths.

Non-Abrahamic Religions

This book is focused on the more than half of humanity, about 3.3 billion people, who share membership in the three Abrahamic faiths. While the creation-evolution debate looms large for many of these people, especially in the United States, this controversy means almost nothing in some of the world's most populous nations: China, India, Japan, Korea, Vietnam, and Thailand.

Nearly a billion of these people follow Hinduism, the world's largest non-biblical tradition. One out of every six people on Earth is a Hindu. Most live in India, where Hinduism is practiced by over 80 percent of the population. Sixty million live outside of India. Over a million live in the United States. Unlike the Abrahamic religions, Hinduism has no founder. Its primary Gods are Brahma (the creator), Vishnu (the protector), and Shiva (the destroyer). All schools of Hinduism share the ideals of happiness for all people, truth, the unity of religions, and the universe as one family. An interesting Hindu belief is that "no particular religion teaches the only way to salvation above all others."

The Veda, Hinduism's Holy Scripture, comprises four books or Vedas, which were written in a language called Vedic, an archaic form of Sanskrit. Some portions of the Vedas were composed over 6,000 years ago and thus predate the book of Genesis and Qur'an. Their contents are said to be preserved exactly as given out by the great Hindu sages of antiquity.

Hinduism has a view of the universe that in many ways is in agreement with modern science; for example, both agree that the *present* universe is about fourteen billion years old. "Present" is emphasized because from the Hindu perspective, universes come and go. There are a variety of Hindu creation stories about how universes come and go. For Hindus, time is without beginning or end. The universe is eternal.

Hinduism believes in the concept of the evolution of life on Earth, but not in the same way it is understood by modern science. According to science, evolving beings have little freedom to determine their evolutionary course in the face of the forces of Nature. Hinduism, on the other hand, while acknowledging that Nature is a powerful agent, says that Nature's effects will continue only so long as individuals are willing to let themselves remain under its influence. Through inner transformation and purification of the mind and body, individuals are said to be able to withdraw from the external world, eliminate all forms of desires, and ultimately make a desireless effort through detachment, devotion and self-surrender. Terrestrial evolution in this sense is a path from death to deathlessness, immortality but not survival, escape from a cycle of births and deaths. It is a product of self-effort, a liberation of the self from the bonds of Nature.

During its long history, Hinduism has spawned four other important religions: Buddhism, which was created after Buddha rejected the authority of the Veda and the concept of an immortal soul (376 million members); Jainism, which originated when Mahavir, who lived at the same time as Buddha, also rejected the Veda (4.2 million); Zoroastrianism, which was established after Zoroaster also broke with Hinduism (2.6 million); and Sikhism, which started in the Punjab and combines Hindu and Muslim ideals (23 million).

The list of religious groups also includes: Confucianism (394 million), primal-indigenous (300 million), African traditional and diasporic (100 million), Juche (19 million), Spiritism (15 million), Baha'i (7 million), Shinto (4 million), Cao Dai (4 million), Tenrikyo (2 million), neo-paganism (1 million), Unitarian-Universalism (800 thousand), Rastafarianism (600 thousand) and Scientology (500 thousand). About 1.1 billion Secular/Nonreligious/Agnostic/Atheistic individuals claim no official religion. About a fifth of these are self-proclaimed atheists.

Strangers Among Us

Among the people adhering to Abrahamic and non-Abrahamic religions, there are some who, rather than accepting a world of differing religious views and practices, believe that one true religion—their own—should prevail. Contrary to the idea that religious institutions and the state should be separate, many of these fundamentalists believe religion and politics are inseparable. Further, they often believe that swearing allegiance to their religion requires them to reject other religions as well as the ideas of modern science. Fundamentalism is a global fact. There is fundamentalist Judaism, fundamentalist Christianity, fundamentalist Islam, as well as fundamentalist Hinduism, Buddhism, Sikhism, and Confucianism.

In view of these diverse viewpoints, it is urgent that we all learn to share this planet with people holding different worldviews and ultimate commitments. Otherwise, we may be evolutionarily replaced.

It is our hope that the views offered by the three scientists help replace antagonistic and potentially destructive convictions with rational ones. It is also our hope that by endorsing the idea that science and faith can be reconciled, people may be emboldened to search out additional paths of convergence rather than divergence.

The remedy to ignorance and superstition is free inquiry, for without questioning, there can be no intellectual growth. Indeed, it is dangerous not to question because, by not questioning, believers are vulnerable to propaganda that presents all understandings that a group finds disagreeable as false, and even heretical. Trapped within their religious perspectives, such believers are blinded to the fruits of free inquiry.

Furthermore, unquestioning allegiance promotes a worldview in which strangers become unacceptably dangerous enemies. This in turn can lead to ideologies that sanction destruction of these strangers. From there, it's only a small step to ideologically motivated religicide, the premeditated annihilation of religious groups: 9/11 was certainly not the first time ignorance and superstition led to outrageous acts. Unfortunately, it is unlikely to be the last.

To those of us who value human rights and who define humanity as a community extending beyond national, religious and ethnic boundaries, the destruction of any group has devastating ramifications for our entire species. Defining humankind is not the privilege of one nation or group. It is the prerogative of all human beings.

And so, we,
David E. Kay,
T. O. Shanavas,
Howard Van Till,
Arthur Wiggins
and Charles Wynn,

reaffirm the ideals that Daniel Pearl's mother says her son represented, ideals that every person in every civilized society should aspire to uphold—openness, pluralism, understanding, freedom of inquiry, truth, and respect for people.

Index

Abd-ar-Rahman Muhammed ibn-Khaldun, 152

Abraham, 2, 5, 125, 148, 160

Abrahamic religions, 6, 8, 178, 180

Abu Bakr Muhammed ibn-Arabi, 151

Adam, 8, 95, 102, 124, 127, 128, 138, 144, 145, 146, 148, 149, 150, 155, 156

Adam and Eve, 150, 151, 155

adenine, 69, 76

adenosine triphosphate, 77, 120

Adonai, 5, 96, 112, 117, 123, 124

African traditional, 179

age of the universe, 8, 16, 18, 19, 20, 25

Al-Baari, 138, 140

Al-Biruni, 134, 151, 153, 169, 171

Al-Jahiz, 151

Allah, 5, 6, 7, 132, 158, 163, 165

allele, 71

al-Razi, 145

American Academy of Pediatrics, 9

American alligator, 55

American Association for the Advancement of Science, 1

American Chemical Society, 154

American Scientific Affiliation, 9

amino acids, 68, 69, 142

ammonia, 68, 69

animal embryos, 74

anopheles mosquito, 53

antibiotic-resistant bacteria, 75

antibiotics, 75

Arabia, 7, 133

Argument from Design, 46, 57, 116

Asad, Muhammad, 168, 169, 170, 172

Atlantic Ocean, 26

atomic nuclei, 23, 24

Australopithecus, 28, 125, 126, 142

Baha'i, 179

Barrett, 103, 104, 106

Best Doctors in America, 9

Betelgeuse, 24

About the Contributors

Rabbi David Kay of Congregation Ohev Shalom in Orlando, Florida, a Jewish scientist who received rabbinic ordination from the Jewish Theological Seminary of America, the institution of higher Jewish learning of the Conservative movement, has a B.Sci. in Ecology, Ethology, and Evolution from the University of Illinois at Urbana-Champaign, an M.A. from the Davidson Graduate School of Jewish Education and has studied at the Schechter Institute of Jewish Studies. He has done biomedical research at the University of Chicago Hospitals and Clinics, has been a science teacher at Yeshivah Shearis Yisroel and served as Education Director of the Tree House Animal Foundation of Chicago.

Howard Van Till, Ph.D., a Christian scientist whose religious beliefs are derived from the Dutch Calvinist tradition, is Professor of Physics and Astronomy, Emeritus, at Calvin College in Grand Rapids, Michigan. He is a Founding Member of the International Society for Science and Religion, has served on the Executive Council of the American Scientific Affiliation and is a member of the Editorial Board of Science and Christian Belief. Dr. Van Till is a member of Christ Community Church Exchange (C3Exchange) in Spring Lake, Michigan.

T. O. Shanavas, M.D., a Muslim scientist, is a pediatrician in Adrian, Michigan and member of the Islamic Center of Greater Toledo and the Islamic Society of North America. He is listed in *Best Doctors in America* and is a Fellow in the American Academy of Pediatrics. Dr. Shanavas is a member of the Center for Theology and the Natural Sciences and National Center for Science Education and serves as Vice President of the Islamic Research Foundation International.

About the Editors

Charles M. Wynn, Sr., is Professor of Chemistry at Eastern Connecticut State University. Dr. Wynn's critically acclaimed science trilogy written with co-editor Arthur Wiggins: *The Five Biggest Ideas in Science, Quantum Leaps in the Wrong Direction: Where Real Science Ends and Pseudoscience Begins,* and *The Five Biggest Unsolved Problems in Science* has been translated into eleven languages.

Arthur W. Wiggins is Distinguished Professor Emeritus of Physics and Astronomy at Oakland Community College in Michigan where he was Head of the Department of Physical Sciences. He is the author of *The Joy of Physics*.

ALL THINGS THAT MATTER PRESS ™

FOR MORE INFORMATION ON TITLES AVAILABLE FROM
ALL THINGS THAT MATTER PRESS, GO TO
http://allthingsthatmatterpress.com
or contact us at
allthingsthatmatterpress@gmail.com

Made in the USA
Charleston, SC
12 July 2011